MW00378680

The modern images — and enduring spirit — of railroading become silhouettes as Union Pacific GE Dash 8-40Cs lug coal hoppers across Wyoming's plains, September 24, 1990. Photo: David M. Johnston.

THE SPIRIT OF RAILROADING

A color celebration of North America's trains

Gary W. Dolzall and Mike Danneman

THE SPIRIT OF RAILROADING

Gary W. Dolzall and Mike Danneman

Text:	**Gary W. Dolzall**
Design and layout:	**Mike Danneman**
Editor:	**Bob Hayden**
Assistant Editors:	**George H. Drury, Marcia Stern**
Production Supervisor:	**Lawrence O. Luser**

DUST JACKET: Beneath the skyline of America's traditional railroad capital — Chicago — Amtrak F40PH 240 and the four-car *State House* begin a journey to St. Louis, May 24, 1991. Photo: Mel Finzer.

 Published by Kalmbach Publishing Co., 21027 Crossroads Circle, P. O. Box 1612, Waukesha, WI 53187. Library of Congress Catalog Card Number 91-061897. ISBN: 0-89024-116-3. Printed in Singapore.

PREFACE

THE IDEA WHICH GAVE FORM to the book you now hold was born in the last hours of an April night, pieced together as we traveled on a dark highway, bound home after a day spent along the main line of the Santa Fe in Illinois. Behind us were encounters with a score of trains — intermodals urged on by AT&SF's blue-and-yellow diesels hustling across the Illinois plains at 70 miles per hour; high-tonnage freights clawing up the 1.1 percent grade of Edelstein Hill; Amtrak's silver *Southwest Chief*.

But no single scene was so etched in our minds — or upon our souls — as what we saw at day's end, along the asphalt station platform at Chillicothe, Illinois. Under an orange sky barely still aglow, Santa Fe train 199 — the hottest piggyback on a hot railroad — hurried west into Chillicothe. The train's big EMD units settled to idle, its string of piggybacks heeled to the clasp of brake shoes, slowing to a pace of a few miles per hour — but not stopping.

At the time, Chillicothe was a crew-change point for conductors and brakemen, but not engineers, and as the train crept past the platform, the crewmen who had manned 199 from Chicago swung off and their replacements carefully stepped aboard. As this human exchange was being completed, the engineer released the brakes and opened the throttle wide. With the deep cry of 12,000 reawakened diesel horsepower, under a torrent of black exhaust and glowing sparks set against the twilight sky, Santa Fe 199 departed Chillicothe just as it had come: in a fury that promised its cargo would arrive in Richmond, California — 45 hours and 2,200 miles later — on time.

What the urgent passing of AT&SF 199 that evening showed us was steel and human evidence that railroading remains alive in spirit and rich in drama. We first explored contemporary railroading in *Steel Rails Across America* (Kalmbach Books, 1989). Now we expand our coverage north to Canada and present more images of railroading. It illustrates the constant pace of change on the railroad scene that many subjects in this book — such as Santa Fe's reborn Warbonnet diesel livery; third-generation, wide-nose diesels on Union Pacific and Burlington Northern and Soo and Conrail; and CP Rail operating the Delaware & Hudson — did not exist two short years ago when our previous book was completed.

This book is intended to capture the spirit and trackside verve of railroading, rather than to offer a definitive coverage of the industry — a task far beyond the scope of 196 pages. Likewise for brevity, we must assume the reader has some familiarity with railroading and its sometimes unique and complicated nomenclature and its penchant for abbreviations. For those who are new to railroading or wish further background information, we recommend Kalmbach's series of contemporary reference guides, particularly *The Train-Watcher's Guide to North American Railroads*, *American Shortline Railway Guide*, *Diesel Locomotive Rosters: U. S., Canada, Mexico*, and *Contemporary Diesel Spotter's Guide*.

Travel with us now as we explore railroading in the modern age, railroading stretching from Florida to British Columbia to Alaska. Join us as we seek to discover the enduring spirit of railroading.

Gary Dolzall, Bethel, Connecticut
Mike Danneman, Butler, Wisconsin
August 1991

To Mark,
a brother and friend.
We cherish the times we shared.

CONTENTS

PREFACE 5

DEDICATION 6

1 THE SPIRIT OF RAILROADING 8
More than simply transportation

2 STEEL TITANS 26
North America's nine tonnage heavyweights

3 TONNAGE AND DIVERSITY 42
The foot soldiers of freight railroading

4 SILVERED VARNISH 58
Railroading's grand tradition

5 THE HEAVY HAULERS 76
Freight railroading's bond with the land

6 THE FAST FLEET 96
Dueling the trucking industry, head on

7 HIGH TECH 110
The faces of dieseldom's third generation

8 STEAM'S SURVIVORS 128
Why the book on steam never closed

9 RAILS IN THE CITIES 140
High drama in grand urban theaters

10 MOUNTAIN RAILROADING 154
Titanic battles fought amid magnificent beauty

11 RAILS ACROSS THE CONTINENT 174
Captivating scenes and changing moods

ACKNOWLEDGMENTS 194

8028
8028
8

1 THE SPIRIT OF RAILROADING

More than simply transportation

THERE IS IN RAILROADING a spirit that calls to the human mind and heart. Timeless and boundless, it first appeared on September 27, 1825, in Yorkshire, England, when Stockton & Darlington's 0-4-0 *Locomotion* turned its drivers to haul 33 cars, introducing to the world what longtime TRAINS magazine editor David P. Morgan coined "The Railway Idea."

Ever since its birth, railroading has called to the human soul. This was true in 1830, when the Baltimore & Ohio, North America's first common-carrier railroad, sent forth its first revenue train. It was true when a golden spike driven at Promontory, Utah, on May 10, 1869, first linked America's Atlantic and Pacific shores. It was true on November 7, 1885, when an iron spike was pounded home at Craigellachie, British Columbia, completing Canada's first transcontinental railroad. It was true during World War II, when North American railroading answered its greatest challenge. And it is true today.

LEFT: Set against the Montana Rockies, Burlington Northern SD40-2 8028 challenges Marias Pass, exemplifying the spirit of railroading. Photo: Tom Danneman. ABOVE: Union Pacific diesels and double-stacks pause at Reverse, Idaho, awaiting a highball signal. Photo: Blair Kooistra.

At Stryker, Ohio, where the look of railroading was once that of New York Central Hudsons, GE diesels and eastbound stacks now are the face — and the fury — of modern railroading on the 13,000-mile Conrail system, June 17, 1989. Photo: Gary W. Dolzall.

Railroading presents different images to each generation, yet maintains its hold on mind and heart. In 1938, when Lucius Beebe's *High Iron* first introduced railroading as a subject worthy of book-length photojournalism, the face of railroading was steam and varnish — swift Pennsylvania K4 Pacifics; diminutive Rio Grande 2-8-2s treading rails set three feet apart; olive-green heavyweights lettered with the respected name "Pullman." Now, the faces are remolded, but the tug of railroading upon the imagination remains firm.

The faces of railroading in the final decade of the 20th century are of angular behemoths built by General Electric and General Motors, diesels bearing designations like Dash 8-40C and SD60; of tall, silver Amtrak Superliners; of stack trains toting multicolored containers; of serpentine unit coal trains. Every day sees proof positive of railroading's undimmed spirit: the determined march of Santa Fe warbonnet-clad GP60Ms and a transcontinental piggyback across Arizona's Aubrey Valley; the sizzling, 100-mph passing of an Amtrak AEM7-hauled "Metroliner" under the graceful catenary of the Northeast Corridor; Burlington Northern diesels lugging 10,000 tons of Power River Basin coal toward the fires of hungry power plants; the slow, captivat-

Autumn's tranquility: Near the southern end of the modest (131 miles) but captivating Vermont Railway, GP38-2 202 leads a freight across the Walloomsac River at North Hoosick, New York, October 8, 1990. Photo: Scott Hartley.

ing wanderings of a pair of bright red Vermont Railway Geeps, toting a handful of freight cars through the Green Mountains; a Conrail double-stack headed by 4,000-horsepower GE diesels, shattering the Saturday afternoon quiet of a tiny Ohio town with its mile-a-minute fury; and the inspiring beauty of crisp red Canadian Pacific SD40-2s cast against the stone peaks of the Rockies.

The railroad scene of the 1990s is dominated by nine steel titans, America's "Super Seven" freight railroads — Burlington Northern, Conrail, CSX, Norfolk Southern, Santa Fe, Southern Pacific, and Union Pacific — and Canada's transcontinental freight giants — Canadian National and Canadian Pacific Rail. The fabric is interwoven with more than 400 other freight haulers — companies as diverse as 6,300-mile Class 1 Chicago & North Western, short (357 miles) but muscular ore-hauler Duluth, Missabe & Iron Range, and the 28-mile Magma Arizona. The railroad scene is made whole by properties entrusted to carry not tonnage, but us: Amtrak, Canada's VIA Rail, and a growing profusion of commuter railroads with names like Metro-North and Metra and GO Transit.

Today's railroading recalls traditions and scenes nearly as old as the industry itself — freight carted in boxcars and hoppers; anxious passengers pacing station platforms; semaphore signals; timber trestles; rails gracefully tracing the banks of North America's great rivers; an engineer's gloved hand on the throttle; a brakeman swinging down to throw a switch; skilled workmen tending locomotives in brick backshops; a conductor punching tickets; and, yes, even steam locomotives (albeit if only for excursion trains and tourist operations) known by initials and numbers such as UP 844 and N&W 1218 and SP 4449.

And yet, railroading increasingly embraces high technology — double-stacks and piggybacks and RoadRailers and the massive, mechanized intermodal terminals that assemble them; micro-processor-equipped diesels; 90-mph push-pull passenger

Mixing new and old, CSX GE Dash 8-40C 7643 attains Sand Patch, Pennsylvania, October 27, 1990, cresting the ancient Baltimore & Ohio crossing of the Alleghenies with westbound tonnage. Photo: Ron Flanary.

Returning empty hoppers to the Powder River Basin for more coal, Chicago & North Western EMD SD60s roll west across the plains of Nebraska. The site is on Union Pacific's main line near North Platte, July 2, 1988. Photo: Mike Danneman.

trains; satellite-assisted signal systems; computerized dispatching centers; and console-equipped, air-conditioned locomotive cabs.

As it always has, today's railroading impresses by its sheer size, whether it be the 3,800 horsepower of a 71-foot-long SD60, the 1,040-foot length of ancient Starrucca Viaduct, the million pounds of Union Pacific Challenger 3985, or the 9.1 miles of Canadian Pacific's Mount McDonald Tunnel . . . or simply the scope of the industry's daily task.

If the intangible spirit and the hard statistics of railroading seem opposites, surely they share one trait — often they dare the imagination. For instance: In the U. S. and Canada, railroads spin more than 200,000 route miles; employ over a quarter-million men and women; and operate more than 20,000 locomotives to haul over a million freight cars. Amtrak carries 22 million passengers a year; VIA (before its 1990 service reductions) 6 million; commuter lines truly staggering numbers (Metro-North moves over 50 million commuters a year). And the freight railroads? Each year, they tote a billion and a half tons, carry more than 6 million piggyback trailers and containers, and generate a trillion revenue ton-miles (one ton of freight hauled one mile). Yes, that's a trillion. In 1988, for the first time America's Class 1 railroads produced that landmark statistic, then repeated it the following year. (At the height of World War II — in 1944 — America's railroads tallied 733 million ton-miles.)

The message in these statistics is reflected in railroading's modern images: A yellow-faced CSX GE Dash 8-40C clawing its way to the summit of the Alleghenies, Union Pacific diesels hustling stacks across the high plains of Wyoming, Burlington Northern hauling tonnage through Montana's Marias Pass, Amtrak Turboliners gliding at 80 mph along the Hudson River, and Canadian National diesels charging across the plains of Manitoba.

More than a century and a half after its birth, the railroad industry still has the vigor to bind the vast North American continent together — and it has the timeless spirit to draw us trackside, to witness the special drama we call railroading.

SP

PRECEDING PAGES: A trio of Southern Pacific EMD diesels curls freight through the magnificent Cascade Mountains, near the summit of SP's Cascade line, at Abernethy, Oregon, March 3, 1989. Photo: James A. Speaker.

Double-track drama: At Williamsfield, Illinois, March 11, 1989, Santa Fe GP50 3811 and its 70-mph hotshot piggyback train 991 run wrong-main to slip past GP60 4002 and its slower-moving eastbound tonnage. Photo: Gary W. Dolzall.

ABOVE: In one of the grandest displays of modern railroading, Burlington Northern drags millions of tons of coal east from Wyoming's Powder River Basin. Here BN C30-7 5528 and kin tame Nebraska's Crawford Hill on July 2, 1989. BELOW: Rio Grande GP40-2 3122 leaves Denver behind as it climbs toward the Rockies with a *RailBlazer* piggyback, July 9, 1989. Both photos: Mike Danneman.

Near the easternmost reaches of railroading on the North American continent, Canadian National 2119 — a rare Bombardier (Montreal Locomotive Works) HR616 — heads tonnage at Iona, Nova Scotia. Photo: Robert Palmer.

ABOVE: Framed by a silver signal bridge, three EMD units lead Norfolk Southern train 187 at Oakdale, Tennessee, on NS's traffic-rich and fabled ex-Southern Railway Cincinnati-Chattanooga "Rathole" main line, October 8, 1989. Photo: Ron Flanary.

LEFT: Wearing what is arguably the most famous face in all of railroading — Santa Fe's red-and-silver Warbonnet livery — AT&SF GP60M 135 ushers piggyback train 188 west through Arizona's Aubrey Valley near Seligman, September 24, 1990. Intermodals are key to 11,700-mile AT&SF's future. Photo: Steve Patterson.

On a steel trail of Western Pacific heritage, three Union Pacific third-generation diesels cross the Great Salt Lake at Ellerbeck, Utah, March 3, 1990. UP acquired WP in 1982. Photo: Dave Gayer.

6726
6726
CONRAIL

409
409
Amtrak

UPPER LEFT: Conrail train TV-500 (TV stands for "trailer van") behind SD50 6726 leans into a curve near Otis, Indiana, bound for Chicago on CR's busy ex-NYC main. Photo: Mike Danneman. BELOW LEFT: Amtrak's Boston-Washington *Patriot* hurries through West Mystic, Connecticut, February 10, 1991, on a segment of the Northeast Corridor often overshadowed by the more bustling, electrified Washington-New Haven (Connecticut) line. Once part of the New Haven, this line is now owned by Amtrak. Photo: Gary W. Dolzall. ABOVE: Four CSX diesels — all still dressed in Chessie System colors — cross the Potomac River at Harpers Ferry, West Virginia, November 4, 1989. Photo: Alan Tillotson.

Santa Fe
Santa Fe
SF

LEFT: Second-generation EMD diesels draw piggybacks over one of Santa Fe's most famous landmarks — 220-foot-deep Canyon Diablo — near Winslow, Arizona, April 19, 1990. Photo: Mike Danneman. ABOVE: Snuggled deep in another of the West's best-known locations — Donner Pass — Southern Pacific SD45 7449 draws tonnage east at snowy Blue Canon, California, in March 1989. Photo: Ron Flanary.

302
302

ABOVE LEFT: As we watch from Bear Mountain Bridge, Amtrak's Turboliner-equipped, New York City-bound *Niagara Rainbow* slips along the east bank of the Hudson River at Anthonys Nose, New York, November 4, 1990. Photo: Gary W. Dolzall. BELOW LEFT: Trailing stubby cars loaded with copper ore, three Copper Basin Railway EMDs clear the rock tunnel near Ray Junction, Arizona, February 20, 1989. The regional Copper Basin Railway was formed from Southern Pacific's Hayden Branch in 1986. Photo: Reid McNaught. BELOW: Two traditions of the 140-year-old Illinois Central Railroad — black locomotives and grain-hauling — are recalled as IC SD20 2005 heads a Chicago-Memphis freight at Chebanse, Illinois, January 21, 1989. Photo: Gary W. Dolzall.

CONRAIL
QUALITY

2 STEEL TITANS

North America's nine tonnage heavyweights

ACROSS THE GRAND EXPANSE of the United States and Canada nine steel titans dominate the railroad scene. Their polished steel paths stretch from Florida to California, from Nova Scotia to British Columbia. In the U. S., seven tonnage-hauling giants — the "Super Seven" — account for roughly 127,000 miles of steel and earn more than two-thirds of U. S. railroading's annual revenues of $25 billion. In Canada, two great transcontinentals stretch across the land, together casting more than 37,000 miles of rails between Atlantic and Pacific.

The roll call of America's Super Seven is both rich in history and fresh born of mergers, consolidations, even bankruptcies. Santa Fe, smallest of the seven, is the oldest, born in 1859. Union Pacific, chartered by Congress in 1862, laid its rails across the West to meet Central Pacific in May 1869 at Promontory; Southern Pacific is descended directly from Central Pacific.

LEFT: Along the west shore of the Hudson River at Fort Montgomery, New York, Conrail Dash 8-40CWs act out the drama of big-time railroading. Photo: Gary W. Dolzall. ABOVE: Santa Fe hotshots meet in the Tehachapi Mountains at Bealville, California. Photo: George W. Hamlin.

Two trademarks of 17,500-mile Norfolk Southern — black, "Thoroughbred" diesels and loaded coal hoppers — are on display as NS train 535 rolls over the Tennessee River, November 18, 1990, at Loudon, Tennessee. Photo: Steve Glischinski.

The rest of the seven are fresher faces. Burlington Northern was born in 1970 in the merger of Chicago, Burlington & Quincy; Great Northern; Northern Pacific; and Spokane, Portland & Seattle. The U. S. government formed Conrail in 1976, piecing together a railroad from bankrupt eastern carriers — Penn Central, Erie-Lackawanna, Reading, Lehigh Valley, and several others. CSX Transportation is the result of the 1980 marriage of Seaboard System and Chessie System. The 1982 linking of Norfolk & Western and Southern Railway forged the "thoroughbred," Norfolk Southern.

Canada's transcontinental giants are equally diverse in their origins. CP Rail traces its Canadian Pacific name back to 1881 and to the iron spike driven at Craigellachie in 1885. Canada's government formed Canadian National in 1922, melding together CN's troubled predecessors under circumstances not unlike those of Conrail a half-century later. Through control of subsidiaries (including Grand Trunk Western and Central Vermont by CN; Soo Line and Delaware & Hudson by CP Rail), these Canadian giants extend their influence across much of the northern tier of the U. S.

Regardless of their histories, today's titans share the trait of having been reshaped by events of the last decade. Foremost among these is the competitive fire of railroad deregulation and the mergers and spin-offs it has forged. Most notable: Union Pacific's growth, accomplished through acquisition of Western Pacific and Missouri Pacific in 1981 and absorption of Katy in 1988, to cover the entire West from Washington and California to Texas and Illinois; Burlington Northern's 1980 merger with Frisco

Coal hoppers trail a trio of UP SD60Ms on Union Pacific's Salt Lake City-Los Angeles steel artery. The site is Sloan, Nevada, 19 miles west of Las Vegas, January 24, 1990. Photo: Mark R. Wayman.

Twisting through the horseshoe at Mance, Pennsylvania, CSX EMDs lift stacks over the Alleghenies, October 20, 1990. Of CSX's 19,300 route miles, perhaps none is more famous than this ex-B&O mountain crossing called Sand Patch Grade. Photo: Mike Danneman.

Just 14 miles out of Canadian National's western terminus of Vancouver, CN SD40s tug covered hoppers across the Fraser River at New Westminster, British Columbia, April 12, 1988. Photo: Mel Finzer.

Life comes briefly to the harsh southeast Arizona desert on SP's Sunset Route as four GE Dash 8-40Bs (lettered for Southern Pacific subsidiary Cotton Belt) roar by at Pantano, Arizona, February 18, 1989. Photo: Reid McNaught.

(St. Louis-San Francisco); Conrail's extraordinary transformation from government ward to privately held, highly respected profit-maker; and Southern Pacific's 1988 melding with Rio Grande and (through subsidiary Cotton Belt) its long-sought extension to America's railroad capital, Chicago, in 1989.

The steel titans share another trait, embodied in CSX diesels grinding tonnage through the mountains of eastern Tennessee; in Southern Pacific intermodals hustling along the Sunset Route through Arizona's desert; in Conrail's mammoth classification yards at Selkirk and Elkhart and Avon; in Santa Fe piggybacks speeding through the gently folded hills of northeast Missouri; in Canadian National rolling tonnage across the endless plains of Alberta. These great railroads share the glamor of big-time, tough-fisted mainline railroading — glory enough to call us to trackside.

White-faced GP39E 2902 wears the 1990s look of America's largest railroad — 28,900-mile Burlington Northern — as it hustles Twin Cities-Chicago *Expediter* train 42 along the Mississippi at Savanna, Illinois, October 13, 1990. Photo: Mike Danneman.

Cajon Pass: Santa Fe and Union Pacific trains meet on Cajon's east slope at Lugo, California, July 22, 1989, proof positive of the giants' shared trackage agreement through the famed pass. Photo: H. Michael Yuhas.

Canadian Pacific SD40-2 5800 exits one of North America's engineering marvels — the spiral tunnel at Yoho, British Columbia — as its own trailing grain hoppers glide overhead. CP built two such spirals at Kicking Horse Pass to tame the Canadian Rockies. Photo: Alex Mayes.

At Mojave, California, five Southern Pacific high-horsepower hood units battle tonnage and the unforgiving desert, April 8, 1990. This SP route, shared with the Santa Fe, crosses both the desert and the Tehachapi Mountains and forms a critical rail link between Southern California and the Bay Area. Photo: Mark Danneman.

Six-axle Burlington Northern diesels — one each from GE and EMD — move a train of hoppers westward at Whitman, Nebraska, July 3, 1989. The empty cars are destined for the coalfields of Wyoming's Powder River Basin. Photo: Mike Danneman.

Rio Grande accounts for roughly 2,100 miles of Southern Pacific Lines' 14,600-mile system — and those miles include the challenges of the Colorado Rockies. Here SD40T-2 5379 and five more units lug tonnage through Tennessee Pass, near Minturn, Colorado. Photo: David M. Johnston.

SEABOARD SYSTEM
CSX

3501 3501

LEFT: Many of CSX's predecessor roads, from Chesapeake & Ohio to Louisville & Nashville to Clinchfield, were virtually synonymous with hauling Appalachian coal. CSX SD50s continue the tradition on ex-Clinchfield rails north of Johnson City, Tennessee, November 16, 1990. Photo: Steve Glischinski. LOWER LEFT: Deep in the Appalachians at Pocket, Virginia, Norfolk Southern likewise continues its coal-hauling tradition, as a mine run headed by high-nosed GE B30-7A 3501 gathers loads on former Southern Railway trackage, September 2, 1988. Photo: Ron Flanary.

BELOW: In a setting far removed from the Appalachians, young fishermen wave at a passing Canadian National freight led by a pair of MLW RSC14s near Bridgewater, Nova Scotia. This line links Halifax and Yarmouth, Nova Scotia, often running in sight of the Atlantic. Photo: Scott Hartley.

3086
CP Rail
3086
1046
CP Rail

PRECEDING PAGES: Magnificent Canada! Set against the snowy peaks of the Rockies and the blue waters of Windermere Lake, Canadian Pacific GP38-2s fly white flags on a freight extra at Windermere, British Columbia, June 14, 1987. Photo: James A. Speaker.

The setting sun lends a warm glow to the warbonneted face of Santa Fe FP45 103 as she hurries across the San Joaquin delta at Bixler, California, March 24, 1990. Built to lead the *Super Chief*, 103 now powers hot AT&SF intermodals. Photo: Steve Schmollinger.

ABOVE: On the line that links the Pacific Northwest with the rest of Union Pacific's 21,800-mile system, tonnage curls around the horseshoe at Leonard, Oregon, behind SD40-2 3348, August 4, 1990. Photo: Blair Kooistra. BELOW: Riding the historic sandstone arches of Starrucca Viaduct at Lanesboro, Pennsylvania, Conrail GP40-2 3386 leads stack train TV-303 across CR's Southern Tier Line, March 19, 1987. Photo: Alan Tillotson.

3 TONNAGE AND DIVERSITY

The foot soldiers of freight railroading

IN TWO COUNTRIES DOMINATED by nine huge railroads, it seems unimaginable that the full tally of freight-hauling railroads could still be more than 400. But it is, and like the foot soldiers of a great army, the ranks of railroads behind the titans give the industry strength, diversity, and character.

Largest among these railroads are the U. S. Class 1s which do not merit "Super Seven" status: Chicago & North Western, Soo Line, Grand Trunk Western, Illinois Central, Kansas City Southern, Florida East Coast, and Guilford Industries. (Rio Grande and Cotton Belt are, for all intents and purposes, part of Southern Pacific.) These railroads match their Super Seven kindred in verve if not in size, and the proof is ample: a mile-a-minute FEC piggyback hurtling through Daytona Beach, a C&NW intermodal hustling piggybacks across Iowa, black Illinois Central diesels lugging endless trains of hoppers south through the farmlands of Illinois, or Soo Line diesels curling along the west bank of

ABOVE: At Neenah, Wisconsin, SDL39 590 presents the face of America's biggest regional — 2,000-mile Wisconsin Central. RIGHT: Below wooded bluffs along the Mississippi River, Soo Line SD40 745 treads south at New Albin, Iowa, August 11, 1990. Both photos: Gary W. Dolzall.

745
745
SOO LINE

ABOVE: Uncommon MLW-built M420R 2002 leads tonnage along the Thames River at Gales Ferry, Connecticut, on the 360-mile Providence & Worcester, August 2, 1990. Photo: Alan Tillotson.
BELOW: Changing times. In October 1988, when bankrupt Delaware & Hudson was operated by regional New York, Susquehanna & Western, trains idle at Mohawk Yard, Schenectady, New York. Today, D&H belongs to CP Rail. Photo: Mel Finzer.

On the main line of 2,800-mile Class 1 Illinois Central, black diesels — a GP40 and two GP38s — draw black hoppers south near Danforth, Illinois, June 12, 1990. Photo: Mike Danneman.

the Mississippi River. With the sole exception of Guilford, which was pieced together in the 1980s from Maine Central, Boston & Maine, and Delaware & Hudson (and has since lost Delaware & Hudson to Canadian Pacific because of D&H's bankruptcy), all of the smaller Class 1s are tradition-rich; and all have proven themselves tough, resourceful industry survivors.

Beyond the Class 1s, the diversity multiplies. Regionals (typically a few hundred to a few thousand miles in length), terminal and switching roads (the likes of the Belt Railway of Chicago and Kansas City Terminal), short lines, and industrial roads take on virtually any task, from hauling the lumber of the Pacific Northwest to feeding the blast furnaces of Pennsylvania steel mills to toting grain out of the Dakotas to rushing double-stacks to New Jersey's Atlantic seaports.

Like the Super Seven, indeed, like so much of railroading itself, the medium-sized and small railroads are a remarkable mixture of old companies and newcomers. Maine's 494-mile Bangor & Aroostook dates from 1891; America's biggest regional, 2,000-mile Wisconsin Central, is nearly a century younger than BAR, spun from ex-Soo Line and Milwaukee Road rails in 1987. Canada's British Columbia Railway was created in this century — in 1912 as the Pacific Great Eastern — and has twice since expanded, in the 1950s and 1980s, to stretch roughly 1,300 miles north through Canada's westernmost province. The final spike of the Alaska Railroad was driven by U. S. President Warren G. Harding in 1923; 114-mile Richmond, Fredericksburg & Potomac dates its charter from 1834; and 777-mile IC spin-off Chicago Central is 151 years younger than venerable RF&P.

North America's regionals, terminal roads, and, particularly, its short lines give railroading a comprehendable, friendly face, and provide train-watchers with uncommon operations in memorable settings. The smaller roads, too, often provide havens for ancient motive power — Alco, Baldwin, and old EMD diesels — no longer wanted on the big properties, but locomotives that are useful and cherished by train-watchers.

The images of railroading beyond the steel titans are both numerous and diverse. They include the polished, never-quiet steel freeway of Chicago's Indiana Harbor Belt, trod by everything from IHB's diminutive diesel switchers to Conrail's burly GE Dash 8-40Cs; the aging but brightly colored Geeps of Florida's Seminole Gulf, carefully stepping across spindly timber trestles; Tacoma Municipal Belt Line's red-and-white Electro-Motive switchers scooting along the docks among great seagoing ships; Monongahela's gray GE diesels dragging coal from the mines of western Pennsylvania; the Alcos of Vermont's Lamoille Valley tiptoeing carefully through the railroad's storybook covered bridge; Montana Rail Link twisting heavy freights up and over Bozeman Pass on on the old Northern Pacific; California's Amador Central keeping its pair of Baldwin diesels busy tugging boxcars; BC Rail's six-axle diesels threading the magnificent Fraser River Canyon; and Erie Mining's F units drawing taconite to the ore docks of Lake Superior.

Surely, the grand menagerie of North America's freight railroads, large and small, remains enough to occupy — and captivate — the train-watcher for a lifetime.

LEFT: Brightly colored Geeps of 106-mile Seminole Gulf cross the timber trestle over Shell Creek near Cleveland, Florida, March 3, 1989. The short line operates two former Atlantic Coast Line branches. Photo: Scott Hartley. ABOVE: GP30s of regional Fox River Valley Railroad roll north past autumn's harvest at Kewaskum, Wisconsin, September 22, 1989. Like the diesels, the trackage is ex-C&NW. Photo: Gary W. Dolzall. BELOW: Alco RS3s of the Lamoille Valley tread lightly through the line's covered bridge at Wolcott, Vermont. Photo: Alan Tillotson.

ABOVE: Dwarfed by oceangoing ships, Tacoma Municipal Belt SW9 1201 works the Tacoma (Washington) waterfront in October 1989. Owned by the city, the road operates 25 miles of track. Photo: Ben Bachman. BELOW: Snuggled against the Sea to Sky Highway, BC Rail MLW M630 710 leads tonnage through Porteau, British Columbia, 26 miles from North Vancouver. Photo: Mel Finzer.

ABOVE: Hustling toward the south end of the 167-mile Duluth, Winnipeg & Pacific, SD40 5907 pounds the crossing of the Duluth, Missabe & Iron Range at Spruce, Minnesota, October 1, 1989. Control of DW&P by Canadian National is evident in the trailing power. Photo: Mike Danneman.
BELOW: Richmond, Fredericksburg & Potomac GP40s ride high at Neabsco, Virginia, rolling train 409 along RF&P's historic 114-mile main line. Photo: Robert Palmer.

In the brick canyons of downtown Kansas City, Missouri, September 16, 1990, Class 1 (C&NW) meets regional (Gateway Western) on the rails of a switching road (Kansas City Terminal). Gateway Western, which operates between Kansas City and St. Louis, was formed from the short-lived regional Chicago, Missouri & Western in 1990. Photo: Mike Danneman.

ABOVE: Guilford (Boston & Maine) second-generation Geeps cross the Hudson River at Mechanicville, New York, August 26, 1989. Once a 4,000-mile system, Guilford has shrunk to roughly 2,300 miles. Photo: Alan Tillotson. BELOW: At Johnsonburg, Pennsylvania, EMD units of 65-mile Knox & Kane, 149-mile Allegheny, and 373-mile Buffalo & Pittsburgh mingle. Photo: John S. Murray.

305
250
250
250

103
103

UPPER LEFT: Stretching across much of Montana and west into Idaho, regional Montana Rail Link was formed in 1987 from ex-BN lines. MRL SD40 250 leads tonnage along the old Northern Pacific main on the west slope of Bozeman Pass, July 27, 1990. Photo: Tom Danneman. LOWER LEFT: Four GP9s of 40-mile Montana Western depart Garrison, Montana, October 5, 1989. Bound for Butte on former NP track, the train consists of interchange traffic from Montana Rail Link. Photo: Dave Gayer. ABOVE: At the north end of 1,600-mile Kansas City Southern, white-faced KCS SD40-2 633 rolls southbound across Gregory Viaduct at Kansas City, Missouri, September 15, 1990. Photo: Tom Danneman.

84
82

281
281

Alcos! Although the Schenectady (New York) builder ceased new locomotive production in 1969, the images of Alcos remain. ABOVE: Five Apache Railroad C420s charge south through the Arizona desert near Holbrook, May 9, 1989. Photo: Steve Glischinski. LOWER LEFT: Pitted against the snows of Michigan, Detroit & Mackinaw C425 281 grinds through Mullett Lake, February 8, 1989. Photo: Ron Cady. BELOW: A quartet of Alcos headed by C420 48 handles Arkansas & Missouri tonnage at Chester, Arkansas, August 28, 1989. Photo: Steve Glischinski.

ABOVE: EMD units from 935-mile Class 1 Grand Trunk Western substitute for BN green diesels on tonnage westbound at Neponset, Illinois, on BN's busy Chicago-Galesburg main line, February 17, 1990. RIGHT: On the Chicago-Twin Cities route that once hosted Chicago & North Western's most famous passenger train — The *400* — C&NW SD50 7006 and a sister head freight across Wisconsin at North Lake, March 30, 1991. Both photos: Mike Danneman.

7006
7006
CNW

273
273
Amtrak
Amtrak

4 SILVERED VARNISH

Railroading's grand tradition

VARNISH: TO TRAIN-WATCHERS the term implies passenger trains, its origin dating from the 19th century when railway cars were varnished wood, inside and out. In the modern context varnished wood has been replaced by stainless steel, but the historical term remains fitting, because nothing else, no matter how modernized, recalls railroading's grand tradition and its enchanting spirit more than passenger trains.

On today's railroads, passenger railroading implies public support. Private-sector freight railroads deemed their passenger trains unprofitable by the mid 1960s. The era of national subsidies began in earnest in the U. S. with Amtrak's formation on May 1, 1971, and in Canada when VIA Rail was created on January 12, 1977. Public support is also the rule in North America's cities, where over the past decade and a half, virtually all commuter operations have been either subsidized or fully assumed by regional transportation authorities.

LEFT: Amtrak's New York-Charlotte *Carolinian* crosses North Carolina's Haw River on Norfolk Southern rails, October 5, 1990. Photo: Mike Small. ABOVE: A traditional and time-honored scene of passenger railroading at Las Vegas, Nevada. Photo: David R. Busse.

Government involvement has, on occasion, reduced or dismantled passenger service (Canada's January 1990 cuts in the VIA Rail system being perhaps the most drastic), but more often it has helped to refurbish or restore equipment and routes rendered weak by years of red ink.

In more than a dozen big U. S. and Canadian cities, commuter railroads deliver trainloads of passengers to work at dawn and bring them home at dusk: Long Island, Metro-North, and New Jersey Transit around New York City; Massachusetts Bay Transportation Authority (MBTA) in Boston; Shore Line East in New Haven, Connecticut; Maryland Rail Commuter (MARC) in Washington and Baltimore; Southeastern Pennsylvania Transportation Authority (SEPTA) in Philadelphia; Tri-Rail in Miami; Metra in Chicago; CalTrans in San Francisco; GO Transit in Toronto; and Montreal Urban

GO Transit F40PH 514 leads a string of GO's unusual Hawker Siddeley bi-levels through Toronto's maze of trackage. GO Transit operates commuter service on more than 200 miles of Canadian National and Canadian Pacific rails. Photo: Alan Tillotson.

ABOVE: MARC AEM7 4903 pushes train 409 south on its morning Baltimore-Washington, D. C., run over Amtrak's Northeast Corridor at Grove, Maryland, June 17, 1987. Photo: Alex Mayes. BELOW: Painted to honor the old New Haven, Metro-North FL9 2002 sleeps away the night at Danbury, Connecticut, April 11, 1991. Four MNCR FL9s owned by Connecticut's Department of Transportation wear this NYNH&H livery. Photo: Gary W. Dolzall and Mike Danneman.

Community Transportation Commission (MUCTC) in Montreal.

For train-watchers — and, more important, for the passengers and commuters — transport by rail now implies carriages as diverse as Amtrak's Superliners and Horizon Fleet and Amfleet and Turboliners; Metra's Budd-built bilevel gallery commuter cars; NJT's Jersey Arrow electrics; VIA's LRCs; Long Island's m.u. electrics; MBTA's Kawasaki double-deckers; and MARC's Budd RDCs. It implies all kinds of motive power, too: state-of-the-art (GO Transit's F59PH diesels and NJ Transit's ALP44 electrics), modern (F40PH diesels on Amtrak, VIA, MBTA, Metra, NJ Transit, and CalTrans), aged (Metro-North and Amtrak FL9s, Metra/Burlington Northern E9s, and MARC F9s), and, indeed, ancient (the boxcab electrics of MUCTC's Canadian National-operated Montreal suburban services). And it implies the aging, sometimes dowdy, sometimes elegant surroundings of Washington Union Station and New York's Grand Central Terminal, Chicago Union Station and Los Angeles Union Passenger Terminal — and of hundreds of small-town station stops from St. Albans, Vermont, to Galesburg, Illinois, to Prince George, British Columbia.

Although North American passenger railroading can't compare with either the volume or diversity of the continent's freight activity, there remain remnants of the era when intercity passenger trains wore every hue. The Alaska Railroad still dispatches

On CSX (ex-B&O) rails, MARC F9PHs pause at Point of Rocks, Maryland, June 13, 1989, with train 269 bound from Washington, D. C., to nearby Brunswick, Maryland. To the left of the station is B&O's old main to Baltimore. Photo: Gary W. Dolzall.

ABOVE: Three burly GE P30CHs lead Amtrak's Virginia-Florida *Auto Train* south over Aquia Creek on the Richmond, Fredericksburg & Potomac, July 23, 1989. Photo: Steve Glischinski. BELOW: In Chicagoland, Metra F40C 600 crosses the Fox River at Elgin, Illinois. Photo: Dan Pope.

ABOVE: Formed in 1980, San Francisco's commuter railroad — CalTrans (its equipment is lettered CalTrain) — acquired 18 F40PH-2s in 1985, including San Jose-bound 911. Photo: Don R. Flynn.
BELOW: On foggy March 1, 1987, a fisherman and his dog witness the passing of Amtrak's Oakland-Bakersfield *San Joaquin* at Middle River, California. Photo: Mike Danneman.

A New Jersey Transit GP40P built for the Central Railroad of New Jersey hurries three coaches over the Manasquan River at Brielle, New Jersey, August 2, 1988, on the old New York & Long Branch. Photo: Alan Tillotson.

scheduled passenger trains that bear its name — as do Canadian regional roads Algoma Central, British Columbia Railway, and Ontario Northland. Albeit with state support, America's last interurban — the Chicago South Shore & South Bend — still hurries electrics east from the Windy City and across northern Indiana. Big roads, from Santa Fe to BN to Conrail, run executive and inspection trains — and often host excursions; small roads from the Green Mountain Railway to Blue Mountain & Reading to California Western haul tourists as well as tonnage. Dinner trains roll across states as diverse as Rhode Island and Iowa and Washington; and in its plush diners and sleepers, the Chicago-Washington-New York *American European Express* brings the prestige and opulence of a cruise ship to steel wheels and steel rails.

In the age of interstate highways and autos and 727s the heated debate about the merits of passenger railroading has continued for much of four decades, and continues yet. We may read of its resolution in the pages of history books yet unwritten, but in this last decade of the 20th century the presence of Amtrak AEM7s whistling along the Northeast Corridor, of Long Island push-pulls hurrying thousands of commuters home to Babylon and Ronkonkoma and Montauk, of the *Sunset Limited*'s Superliners streaking across the high desert of west Texas, of VIA LRC's spinning over the steel speedway between Toronto and Montreal, of CalTrans F40s and bi-levels rushing morning commuters to San Francisco, surely provide evidence that — in deed and in spirit — railroading's silvered varnish is far from dead.

230
230
Amtrak
329

329

PRECEDING PAGES: Leaving an eastbound Santa Fe freight in its wake, Amtrak's Los Angeles-Chicago *Southwest Chief* hurries through Darling, Arizona, on the east slope of AT&SF's Arizona Divide, April 19, 1990. Photo: Mike Danneman.

BELOW: Along the east bank of the Hudson River, Amtrak FL9 489 ducks out of Breakneck Tunnel with the Albany-New York City *Bear Mountain*, in December 1990. This ex-NYC trackage is owned by Metro-North. Photo: Gary W. Dolzall. ABOVE RIGHT: GP49 2807 and GP40-2 3010 of the state-owned Alaska Railroad roll varnish along the Anchorage-Fairbanks main line, crossing Riley Creek trestle in Denali National Park, June 6, 1990. Photo: Steve Glischinski. BELOW RIGHT: Passenger-train drama: Amtrak's *Empire Builders* meet at dusk in snowy Montana, as viewed from the rear of eastbound train 8. Photo: Mike Danneman.

ALASKA

Bombardier-built LRC 6907 powers VIA Rail train 64 at Lachine, Quebec, nine miles west of Montreal on Canadian National's bustling Montreal-Toronto main line, October 19, 1986. Photo: Scott Hartley.

ABOVE: "Ancient" describes Canadian National electrics 6714 and 6713, here powering an MUCTC commuter train on the 17-mile Montreal-Deux Montagnes (Quebec) line, August 30, 1990. Six such boxcabs were built between 1914 and 1916 by General Electric. Photo: Scott Hartley. BELOW: At the halfway point in its round-trip excursion between Sault Ste. Marie, Ontario, and the scenic Agawa River Canyon, Algoma Central GP38-2 205 waits to bring its tourists home. Photo: Mike Danneman.

ABOVE: The Budd RDCs of BC Rail's *Cariboo Dayliner* ride a steel trestle near Lillooet, British Columbia, August 31, 1986. BC Rail operates regular passenger service between North Vancouver and Prince George, British Columbia. Photo: Steve Glischinski. RIGHT: Before its discontinuance in the face of the drastic VIA cuts of January 1990, the *Canadian* was arguably North America's most famous train. West of Exshaw, Alberta, VIA's flagship traces the bank of the Bow River on CP's main line through the Rockies on March 12, 1988. Photo: Mel Finzer.

HIGHLANDS
9904

ABOVE: Named for the Pennsylvania Railroad's flagship, Amtrak's *Broadway Limited* crosses a Pennsy landmark, Rockville Bridge, over the Susquehanna River at Harrisburg, Pennsylvania, February 18, 1991. Waiting behind is a Conrail freight. BELOW LEFT: In pouring rain at Highlands, Illinois, April 13, 1990, Burlington Northern E9s race west out of Chicago with a pair of rush-hour commuter trains. Two photos: Gary W. Dolzall. BELOW: Long Island FA2 control car 602 leads a commuter run past PD Tower at Patchogue, New York, on LIRR's Montauk branch. Photo: Alan Tillotson.

5 THE HEAVY HAULERS

Freight railroading's bond with the land

NORTH AMERICA'S RAILROADS have always performed tough, unforgiving jobs — and for decades the first among these has been hauling coal. Each year U. S. and Canadian railroads move more than a half billion tons of bituminous coal. Deep in the Appalachians, in the coalfields of the Midwest and South, in the rugged Colorado Rockies, in the open grasslands of Wyoming's Powder River Basin, in the Crowsnest coalfields of British Columbia, coal is wrenched from the earth, then carried by rail in virtually every compass direction — to Atlantic and Pacific ports for export, to industries and power plants from New Hampshire to New Mexico.

The railroads which count coal among their major commodities make up a virtual who's who of railroading. Titan Burlington Northern, now North America's biggest coal hauler, each year moves 130 million tons of coal from the Powder River Basin alone; longtime granger road Chicago & North Western, linked with Union Pacific, shares Wyoming's

ABOVE: Four C&NW trains with SD60s on the point meet at Bill, Wyoming, July 4, 1989, with hoppers bound for the coal mines of the Powder River Basin. Photo: Mike Danneman. RIGHT: Two symbols of heavy hauling — coal hoppers and grain elevators — are in evidence as Illinois Central diesels roll through Ashkum, Illinois, May 6, 1990. Photo: Gary W. Dolzall.

ASHKUM
GRAIN CO.
2035

enormous tonnage of black diamonds. Conrail, CSX, and Norfolk Southern, like their predecessors, tug tens of thousands of hopper loads of coal from the mines of West Virginia and Pennsylvania; CN, CP, and British Columbia Railway haul coal from the newer mines of Canada's western provinces. Illinois Central taps the strip mines of southern Illinois, and smaller properties such as Monongahela and Indiana Rail Road and Colorado & Wyoming and Utah Railway survive by hauling hopper loads of coal.

For the train-watcher few sights and sounds are more awesome than a railroad battling coal tonnage. The drama is the same, whether it's BN green diesels set fore and aft on 100 hoppers, lifting 10,000 tons of Powder River Basin coal over Nebraska's Crawford Hill; or Norfolk Southern SD60s and C39-8s drawing endless strings of hoppers east from Bluefield, West Virginia; or Canadian National SD50Fs threading coal trains through the Thompson River Canyon; or Pittsburg & Shawmut coaxing hoppers forward with its elderly EMDs. Dating from when railroads not only hauled coal but burned it in the fireboxes of 0-6-0s and 2-8-2s and 4-8-8-4s, there are few industrial alliances more rich in history than railroading's bond with coal.

While coal dominates North America's railroad

ABOVE: Eastbound coal meets westbound grain on Nebraska's Crawford Hill, July 2, 1989, in big-time Burlington Northern action. The units in the background are pushers on the coal train. Photo: Mike Danneman. BELOW: D&RGW EMDs and coal hoppers curl around the double horseshoe near Crater, Colorado, on Rio Grande's Craig branch, on October 3, 1987. Photo: James A. Speaker.

SD40s tow a grain extra east at Dalemead, Alberta, November 8, 1990, in a classic Canadian granger scene along CP Rail's transcontinental main. Photo: Mel Finzer.

tonnage, the same steel-fisted determination must be brought to the tasks of moving staggering volumes of grain, ore, potash, steel, timber, oil . . . you name it. Other minerals — stone, cement, iron ore, phosphate — account for more than 10 percent of railroading's total tonnage; grain 10 percent; timber and lumber 5 percent.

And for those of us at trackside, the drama created in the hauling of that tonnage is grand: Canadian Pacific SD40-2s tugging 20 million pounds of grain across Alberta; Kansas City Southern SD50s weaving jumbo grain hoppers from America's heartland toward the Gulf of Mexico; maroon Duluth, Missabe & Iron Range six-axle diesels guiding stubby cars of taconite to Lake Superior docks; Conrail dragging coils of steel toward Detroit; Southern Pacific lifting serpentine oil trains over Tehachapi; or CSX diesels rolling dusty gray hoppers of phosphate toward Florida's west shore.

The great and unforgiving chores of hauling bulk commodities bond North American railroading to the soil that its rails cross and crisscross. Heavy hauling is traditional railroading — railroading in its purest form.

ABOVE: On the shore of Lake Erie at Ashtabula Harbor, Ohio, in August 1988, Conrail diesels tend strings of hoppers while a Great Lakes freighter unloads its cargo in the distance. Photo: Mel Finzer.

ABOVE: Hauling grain from America's heartland to Gulf of Mexico ports is a tradition for Kansas City Southern. Here, four KCS EMDs headed by SD50 709 roll covered hoppers through the Ouachita Mountains at Rich Mountain, Arkansas. Photo: David M. Johnston.

BELOW: Mile-for-mile, few haulers in North America take on a heavier task than the coal-carrying 136-mile Monongahela Railway. Once famous for its ex-New York Central Baldwin Sharknose diesels, the road now employs GE "Super" B23-7s such as this pair at Buzz, Pennsylvania, October 14, 1990. Photo: Robert Palmer. RIGHT: Black diesels tote black diamonds as Norfolk Southern GE C39-8 8582 and a sister bark through Raleigh, North Carolina, June 8, 1988. Photo: Mel Finzer.

A trio of CSX GE U18Bs — two still in original Seaboard Coast Line livery — chugs across the Alafia River in East Tampa, Florida. They leave Tampa Bay behind to return to Florida's "Bone Valley" for more phosphate loads, March 4, 1989. Photo: Scott Hartley.

4212
ERIE MINING COMPANY
4212

Autumn in Minnesota ore country. LEFT: Why 73-mile Erie Mining is noted for its diesel roster is clear as a set of EMD F9s and an Alco road-switcher team up to tug ore cars at Cramer, Minnesota, October 7, 1990. Photo: Steve Glischinski. BELOW: At Wales, Minnesota, September 30, 1989, maroon EMDs of fabled 357-mile Duluth, Missabe & Iron Range roll taconite loads toward Lake Superior on DM&IR's Iron Junction-Two Harbors line.
Photo: Gary W. Dolzall.

9246
9246

Powder River Basin coal! LEFT: Burlington Northern SD60Ms and leased Oakway SD60s power an eastbound coal train at Medora, North Dakota, July 28, 1990. This is the former Northern Pacific main line, which serves as part of BN's northern outlet for Powder River Basin coal traffic. Photo: Tom Danneman. BELOW: Sharing the enormous tonnage of the Powder River Basin, Chicago & North Western moves coal through Reno Junction, Wyoming, September 4, 1990, behind two Dash 8-40Cs and an SD60. Photo: Mark R. Lynn. BELOW LEFT: Powder River coal originated by C&NW moves east on Union Pacific's Overland Route. At dusk, July 1, 1989, an eastbound train behind a UP SD60M nears North Platte, Nebraska. Photo: Mike Danneman.

Carrying on 205-mile Bessemer & Lake Erie's long-standing penchant for heavy hauling, B&LE SD38s roll coal loads northbound at Rural Ridge, Pennsylvania, July 4, 1986. Photo: John S. Murray.

On the old Western Pacific at Clifside, October 28, 1989, Union Pacific SD60M 6184 and two Dash 8-40Cs lift westbound coal up Silver Zone Pass through the Toano Range in eastern Nevada. Photo: Dave Gayer.

Two-fisted tradition: Four aged Conrail Geeps move heavily laden gons away from the Bethlehem Steel plant, trudging past rows of hoppers filled with waiting ore and coal at Bethlehem, Pennsylvania. Photo: John S. Murray.

ABOVE: Aluminum hoppers, a steel-and-concrete bridge, and CSX SD50s wearing Seaboard System colors present a contemporary look as coal loads curl around the connection between CSX and Norfolk Southern rails at Big Stone Gap, Virginia. Photo: Ron Flanary. BELOW: Deep in the Appalachians on the old Virginian Railway (hence the catenary poles), a pair of GEs headed by C36-7 8529 leads coal loads over the trestle at Bud, West Virginia. Photo: Dan Pope.

Oil in the West. ABOVE: Providing Shell with a rolling pipeline over the Tehachapi Mountains, SP high-horsepower diesels snake through Caliente, California, March 18, 1989. Such movements transport crude oil from Bakersfield-area wells to the Los Angeles basin for refining. Photo: George W. Hamlin. RIGHT: Union Pacific SD40-2 3379 heads a westbound train of Mobil oil on the old WP at Doyle, California, September 10, 1988. Photo: Steve Schmollinger.

3379
UNION
PACIFIC

ABOVE: Near the shores of the Atlantic Ocean in eastern Nova Scotia at Waverley, Canadian National M630s tug diminutive hoppers heavily loaded with gypsum, May 27, 1987. Photo: Scott Hartley. BELOW: Trailing coal loads that originated on BN, SD38s of 231-mile Elgin, Joliet & Eastern head east around the outskirts of Chicago at Frankfort, Illinois, November 12, 1989. Photo: Mel Finzer.

Grinding out of the Mississippi River valley, six Soo Line EMDs headed by SD40-2 786 depart Marquette, Iowa, April 22, 1990. The train consists of covered hoppers bound for Mason City, Iowa, on this former Milwaukee Road grain artery. Photo: Gary W. Dolzall.

5346
5346
SANTA FE

6 THE FAST FLEET

Dueling the trucking industry, head on

THERE WAS A TIME in railroading when "fast fleet" implied passenger trains, flagship trains named *20th Century Limited* and *Morning Zephyr* and *Super Chief*. In terms of pure speed, passenger trains still hold top honors on this continent and around the world. But given the freight-hauling emphasis of North American railroading, in numbers and importance the fast fleet of today is intermodal traffic — trains that duel the trucking industry, head on.

The concept of piggyback service (carrying truck trailers on flatcars) dates back to the steam era, to Long Island and Nickel Plate and Chicago Great Western. But piggyback was a curiosity when NKP 2-8-4s carted short trailers atop wooden flats, and not until the 1960s did annual piggyback counts exceed 1 million trailers. Today the service and the technology have matured: Trailers and containers are loaded aboard 89-foot steel flats (TOFC and COFC); set upon lightweight, articulated skeleton cars; layered two-high on massive, five-unit articulated double-stack well cars; or even

LEFT: Santa Fe/Conrail coast-to-coast piggyback train Q-LANY howls eastbound through remote Ethel, Missouri, at 8:50 a.m., June 16, 1990. Photo: Gary W. Dolzall. ABOVE: Competitors meet along the Burlington Northern at Earlville, Illinois, February 17, 1990. Photo: Mike Danneman.

ride the rails without flatcars (RoadRailer). Today the benchmark is moving 6 million trailers and containers a year — and the service is growing.

The symbols and names of today's intermodal hotshots evoke images of high-green signals. Conrail has TV trains (for trailer vans), CSX runs its Florida-New Jersey *Orange Blossom Special*, Norfolk Southern operates *RoadRailers*, Burlington Northern has *Expediters*, CN runs *Lazers*. Likewise the fleets of stack trains which carry steamship company names — SeaLand, American President Lines, Evergreen, and Maersk, for instance — all imply time-sensitive cargo, urgency, speed. Nothing illustrates intermodal's stature in the industry better than recent events on Santa Fe, where the most famous railroad livery in the world (AT&SF's red-and-silver Warbonnet passenger colors) and the company's most hallowed train name, "Super" (this time in "Super Fleet"), were resurrected in 1990 and applied to the diesels that haul the road's hot intermodal trains.

At trackside, there is nothing more explosive than the furious passing of an intermodal train, for it combines the bulk and shattering sounds of freight

LEFT: Gliding along on Track 1 of Burlington Northern's three-track Chicago-Aurora (Illinois) raceway, BN train 3 begins its journey to the Pacific Northwest, August 25, 1990. Photo: Gary W. Dolzall. ABOVE: A pair of MLW/Bombardier HR616s and an M630 urge Canadian National intermodal traffic eastbound at Pointe Claire, Quebec, 16 miles west of Montreal. Photo: Scott Hartley. BELOW: Rio Grande SD40T-2 5348 heads a mix of D&RGW and SP units powering stacks and tonnage through the Rockies at Princeton, Colorado, September 2, 1990. Photo: Mark R. Lynn.

service with speeds and efficiency once reserved for varnish. Such is the lesson of an encounter with Burlington Northern train 3 — the road's hotshot Chicago-Seattle piggyback and stack train — blasting out of Chicago behind a white-faced GP30; or an enormous string of American President Lines' double stacks gliding across the Nebraska plains behind Union Pacific Dash 8-40CWs; or SeaLand stacks rolling over Starrucca Viaduct behind Susquehanna Dash 8-40Bs; or Southern Pacific GP60s marching an intermodal up California's Beaumont Hill; or Florida East Coast's deep blue GP40-2s hurtling piggybacks toward Miami; or a Conrail TV climbing the Alleghenies with verve.

A great and urgent challenge faces railroading's fast fleet. To prosper into the next century, to capture business beyond hauling the commodities that have always been its staples, North American railroads must compete with the trucking industry at its own game — speed, service, consistency — and win.

Nearly synonymous in the modern era with intermodal traffic, Florida East Coast shows why as a pair of GP40-2s and a veteran GP9 hustle piggybacks over the Eau Gallie River, four miles north of Melbourne, Florida, January 21, 1990. Photo: Steve Glischinski.

ABOVE: Four Union Pacific Dash 8-40CWs totaling 16,000 horsepower tug eastbound stacks through California's Cajon Pass, September 25, 1990. Photo: Don R. Flynn. BELOW: Racing a thunderstorm on Southern Pacific's Golden State Route, Cotton Belt GP60 9666 hurries stacks and piggybacks west of Vaughn, New Mexico, September 7, 1990. Photo: Mark R. Lynn.

524
524
530
530

9511
9511
anta Fe

PRECEDING PAGES: Santa Fe hot spot. At AT&SF's Belen (New Mexico) servicing facilities, three Santa Fe trains converge under a night sky on May 22, 1991. Heading up two intermodal trains are Santa Fe's newest power — Warbonnet-clad GE Dash 8-40Bs. Photo: Mike Danneman.

ABOVE: On the "Joint Line" shared by D&RGW, BN, and AT&SF, southbound Santa Fe and northbound Burlington Northern intermodal traffic passes at Sedalia, Colorado, July 7, 1989. Photo: Mike Danneman. BELOW: High-nosed Norfolk Southern GP50 7031 hits single track at Bristow, Virginia, August 3, 1990, on the former Southern Railway Washington-Atlanta main line. Photo: George W. Hamlin. RIGHT: Stacks and piggybacks ride below the autumn-hued bluffs of the Mississippi River as Burlington Northern train 3 rolls north of Savanna, Illinois, October 21, 1989. Photo: Gary W. Dolzall.

BELOW: Bound from Kansas City to Chicago with stacks off the Southern Pacific, Soo Line SD60 6057 and a sister hurry across Illinois near Lanark, on former Milwaukee Road rails, April 7, 1990. Photo: Gary W. Dolzall. RIGHT: Stacks stretch in the distance as Union Pacific SD40-2s roll along the Columbia River, near Heppner Junction, Oregon, August 14, 1988. Photo: James A. Speaker.

Chicago & North Western GP50 5050 leads a mix of C&NW and UP power rolling stacks east of Dow City, Iowa, August 27, 1988, on C&NW's once double-tracked Chicago-Omaha main. Photo: Mark Danneman.

Little hindered by a downpour, a westbound Conrail TV train climbs the east slope of the Alleghenies at MG Tower, Pennsylvania, October 21, 1988. The front two units — both SD45-2s — are head-end helpers added for the mountain crossing. Photo: Gary W. Dolzall.

RIGHT: Nestled amid Appalachian foliage, blue-and-gray SD40-2 8134 leads CSX intermodal train R142 along ex-Louisville & Nashville rails at Habersham, Tennessee, in October 1989. Photo: Ron Flanary.

LEFT: Cotton Belt GP60 9693 and two Burlington Northern SD40-2s hustle containers west through the Arizona desert on Southern Pacific's Sunset Route, April 21, 1990. Photo: Mike Danneman. ABOVE: Santa Fe Chicago-Los Angeles piggyback train 198 is nearing its destination as it rolls through Victorville, California, October 20, 1990, behind four "Super Fleet" GE and GM diesels. Photo: Mark R. Wayman.

7 HIGH TECH

The new faces of dieseldom's third generation

HALF A CENTURY AGO DIESELIZATION began in earnest. To borrow a phrase from the late David P. Morgan, "the diesel that did it" was Electro-Motive's FT. Built in 1939, the first FT — olive green and yellow Electro-Motive demonstrator 103 — returned in the summer of 1989 to its LaGrange (Illinois) birthplace and was restored to original form. On September 17, 1989, it was displayed at an open house marking the 50th anniversary of its construction. In all, 16 General Motors diesels — from the first GP7 to a Reading GP30 to a Union Pacific SD60M — stood with FT 103 at LaGrange that day, representing three generations of North American dieseldom.

Yes, three generations. The old diesels of the first generation, Electro-Motive cab units, early Geeps, now-orphaned Baldwins and Alcos and Fairbanks-Morses and Limas which displaced steam, were, in turn, relegated to the shadows by a second generation of diesels — high-horsepower hood units from General Motors, Alco, and General Electric.

ABOVE: From a generation long past, this is the most famous face in dieseldom — Electro-Motive FT 103. Photo: Mike Danneman. RIGHT: Typical of third-generation diesels, Union Pacific GE Dash 8-40CW 9412 heads tonnage at East Garnet, Nevada, December 14, 1990. Photo: Mark R. Wayman.

9412
UNION PACIFIC
9412
60
50

Tonnage snakes along the west bank of the Mississippi River south of Lansing, Iowa, April 22, 1990, behind Soo Line's first third-generation diesel — SD60 6000. Photo: Gary W. Dolzall.

The last of the steam builders that tried its hand at diesels — Alco — is now more than two decades gone (its Canadian cousin, Montreal Locomotive Works/Bombardier, continued to build diesels of Alco design into the 1980s). Only two industrial heavyweights — General Motors (Electro-Motive in the United States; GM Diesel Division in Canada) and General Electric — are left to build the third generation of diesel power.

Locomotive development is often as much evolutionary as revolutionary, and the line between one generation and the next is unclear. But third-generation dieselization clearly implies "high tech" — locomotives with potent, fuel-efficient power plants matched to on-board microprocessors. GE's "Dash 8" series and GM's "Super" 60s, both introduced in 1984, are clearly third-generation machines.

Train-watchers, preoccupied as they may be with the internal details of SD60s and Dash 8-40Cs, gauge locomotives as much by looks as by tonnage ratings, and with the third generation came new faces. At first GM's SD60 and GP60 changed little from their immediate predecessors (the 50-series), retaining the long, straight lines and the squared cab which had become as familiar as GM's F units two generations before. GE's Dash 8s were another story: Gone were the rounded carbodies, cabs, and noses that had characterized GEs from the U25B to the B36-7, and in their place were beveled noses, angular cabs, boxy hoods, massive squared radiators.

ABOVE: The rugged, angular form of GE's Dash 8s is revealed as Norfolk Southern C39-8 8677 and a visiting Conrail Dash 8-40C tug empty hoppers bound for Appalachian mines through Montgomery, Virginia, October 24, 1990. Photo: Mike Danneman. LEFT: The lanky hood of Norfolk Southern SD60 6588 displays NS's "Thoroughbred" image at Andover, Virginia, September 15, 1985. Photo: Ron Flanary.

Paired Conrail SD60s head into the late evening sun, ushering auto racks and mixed tonnage west toward Chicago along CR's ex-New York Central main line at Chesterton, Indiana, June 30, 1990. Photo: Mike Danneman.

GE's Dash 8s were to wear the crown as the most powerful contemporary diesels (up to 4,000 horsepower), and those Dash 8s seemed determined to look the part.

There was more change to come. Variously called the "wide nose," "comfort cab," or "safety cab," this new look originated in Canada in 1974, and became commonplace on Canadian National and British Columbia Railway (CP waited until its SD40Fs of 1988). But aside from a handful of Montreal-built M420s for the Providence & Worcester, the distinctive visage remained outside the U. S. for a decade and a half. Then, a few years into the third generation, came advanced control consoles for engineers and a commitment to bigger, safer, more aerodynamic crew quarters. On SD60Ms for Union Pacific and Soo Line and Burlington Northern; on Dash 8-40CWs for UP and Conrail and CSX; on Warbonnet-clad GP60Ms and Dash 8-40Bs for Santa Fe, this new face quickly appeared across America, from Boston to Barstow.

If microprocessors are a requisite for third-generation diesels, the wide nose is, so far, simply an option. But both microprocessors and wide-noses — one technical, one visual — are changing the face of locomotion and the face of railroading.

Susquehanna Dash 8-40B 4008 and a sister cross the frozen Mohawk River at Schenectady, New York, January 14, 1989. NYS&W operated the Delaware & Hudson before CP Rail's purchase of the D&H. Photo: Scott Hartley.

RIGHT: West of St. Louis at Kirkwood, Missouri, on former Missouri Pacific rails now owned by Union Pacific and shared by Cotton Belt (SP), SSW GP60 9672 heads west with tonnage, June 12, 1990. Photo: Mike Danneman. BELOW: Wide-cab diesels from Electro-Motive and General Electric mingle at San Bernardino, California, September 7, 1990, as AT&SF GP60M 143 meets UP Dash 8-40CW 9369. Photo: Don R. Flynn. FAR RIGHT: The vivid orange nose stripes of Rio Grande GP60 3154 accent Colorado's autumn aspens as an eastbound freight nears the summit of D&RGW's Tennessee Pass, September 22, 1990. Photo: Dave Gayer.

50
40
3154
3154
Grande

RIGHT: Conrail Dash 8-40C 6027 leads three units across New Jersey's Hackensack River at HX Drawbridge, January 13, 1990, with tonnage bound for CR's massive Oak Island (New Jersey) terminal. Photo: Alan Tillotson.

BELOW: This scene could easily be in Iowa, but instead it's in Indiana. On Conrail's ex-NYC Chicago main line at Otis, Chicago & North Western SD60 8016 leads UP diesels and auto racks on June 9, 1990. C&NW (and UP and AT&SF and BN) power frequently operates on this CR line as far east as Elkhart, Indiana. Photo: Mark Danneman.

Candy-apple red Soo Line SD60s led by wide-cab 6058 power train 203 past the north shore of Pewaukee Lake, Wisconsin, October 6, 1990, on the former Milwaukee Road Chicago-Twin Cities main line. Photo: Mike Danneman.

8526

9254
9254

ABOVE LEFT: Doing what they were purchased to do — lug Powder River Basin coal — C&NW Dash 8-40Cs meet at Bill, Wyoming, September 4, 1990. Photo: Mark R. Lynn. LEFT: Displaying the beveled nose and two-piece windshield of SD60Ms delivered to Burlington Northern in 1991, BN 9254 and a sister roll a unit train of potash south along the Mississippi River near Savanna, Illinois, April 27, 1991. Photo: Mike Danneman. ABOVE: First SD60s on Burlington Northern (in 1986) were 100 Oakway leased units dressed in General Motors colors. At Bismarck, North Dakota, July 29, 1990, Oakway SD60 9047 crosses the Missouri River. Photo: Tom Danneman.

101
101
SANTA FE

PRECEDING PAGES: Set against an angry summer sky, two Santa Fe GP60Ms and an FP45 crest the Arizona Divide with AT&SF's Chicago-Los Angeles hotshot piggyback train 188, June 30, 1990. Photo: Mark R. Wayman.

In the last fingers of sunlight on October 7, 1989, leased LMX GE B39-8 8551 leads Burlington Northern train 204 between autumn-colored bluffs and the east bank of the Mississippi River at Victory, Wisconsin. BN leased 100 such GE units beginning in 1987. Photo: Gary W. Dolzall.

Far from home rails, Conrail Dash 8-40CW 6075 leads three GE units powering a CR-Norfolk Southern run-through freight on the NS at Jamestown, North Carolina, November 1, 1990. Photo: Mike Small.

The first General Electric diesels built for mainline service in Canada were 30 wide-nose, cowl-carbody Dash 8-40CMs delivered to Canadian National in 1990. At Caron, Quebec, May 25, 1990, CN Dash 8-40CM 2403 has intermodal traffic in tow as it encounters VIA Rail F40PH-2 6426 on the point of VIA train 30. Photo: Scott Hartley.

809
809

FAR LEFT: Harbinger of the look of the 1990s, General Electric B39-8W test unit 809 was the first GE diesel to feature a modern comfort-cab design. Here she sleeps away the night on the Union Pacific at Las Vegas, Nevada, December 16, 1989. Photo: Mark R. Wayman. ABOVE: Power! Five UP Dash 8-40Cs worth 20,000 horsepower and a trio of older EMDs lead stacks through Cajon Pass, California, December 10, 1989. Photo: David R. Busse. LEFT: The face of contemporary railroading, as exemplified by UP SD60M 6149, reflects off UP's polished rail west of Kearney, Nebraska, July 12, 1990. Photo: Mike Danneman.

8
STEAM'S SURVIVORS

Why the book on steam never closed

ON THAT DAY IN SEPTEMBER 1827 when common-carrier railroading was born in England, odds are that all eyes were focused on Stockton & Darlington 0-4-0 *Locomotion*, simply because locomotives have forever preoccupied train-watchers. Locomotives — especially steam locomotives — have always, by virtue of their bulk and sound and smell and motion, seemed alive. That explains why, even in the third generation of dieselization, steam still polishes the steel rails of North America; why volunteers give their time to renew ancient boilers; why for-profit corporations abide, welcome, even sponsor the iron horse.

For all intents and purposes, mainline railroading closed the book on steam in 1960, when the last stalwarts — Grand Trunk Western, Canadian National, Norfolk & Western, and Illinois Central — dropped their fires for the last time. Logically speaking, the book should have remained closed. But such is the magic of steam that even as it died,

ABOVE: At Elliston, Virginia, Norfolk & Western 1218 and 611 revive the glory of steam for the 1987 National Railway Historical Society Convention. Photo: John S. Murray. RIGHT: Sunset silhouettes the face of Cotton Belt 819 as the 4-8-4 simmers on home rails at Waldenburg, Arkansas, June 17, 1990. Photo: Steve Glischinski.

Famous 4-8-4: A stalwart of the steam scene for three decades, Union Pacific 844 hits her stride during a photo run-by on June 14, 1990. The location is UP's (ex-MP) Chicago-St. Louis main at Hillsboro, Illinois, during the 1990 NRHS convention. Photo: Mike Danneman.

the iron horse began its resurrection. Pennsylvania's 3-foot-gauge East Broad Top, out of work as a coal-hauler since 1956, reopened in 1960 to haul tourists behind steam. Deep in the Colorado Rockies, Rio Grande's 3-foot-gauge lines began a slow transformation from tonnage to tourists. And on the main lines, Reading (1959), Union Pacific (1961), and Burlington (1964) called steam to the high iron for excursion encores. Union Pacific's locomotive was a 4-8-4 numbered 844, and still she steams today.

But the single event which assured steam a place in modern railroading occurred on June 6, 1964, when ex-Southern Railway 2-8-2 No. 4501, purchased by Paul Merriman from the 10-mile Kentucky & Tennessee, steamed down the Southern Railway's busy main line from Stearns, Kentucky, to Chattanooga, Tennessee. Steam had been absent from Southern Railway since 1953, but what followed the run of Southern 4501 — and what yet continues — was a remarkable commitment, first by

ABOVE: South of Pine Bluff, Arkansas, site of the company shops that constructed her in 1943, Cotton Belt 4-8-4 819 cruises on the SSW main and crosses the Saline River, April 21, 1989. Photo: David M. Johnston. BELOW: After a 29-year retirement, Baldwin-built (1926) Frisco 1522 was returned to steam in 1988. On August 14, 1989, the 4-8-2 brings steam's glory to regional Wisconsin Central, rolling south at Colgate, Wisconsin. Photo: Gary W. Dolzall.

Southern Railway, then successor Norfolk Southern, to rekindle the fires of steam.

In the years following the rebirth of 4501 (which still steams at the Tennessee Valley Railroad Museum), the Southern Railway sponsored locomotives as uncommon and endearing as a Savannah & Atlanta 4-6-2, a Texas & Pacific 2-10-4, and a Chesapeake & Ohio 2-8-4. Successor Norfolk Southern today stables two of the family's glorious own — Norfolk & Western J-class 4-8-4 611 and massive A-class articulated 2-6-6-4 1218.

In the 30 years since steam was replaced by diesels in revenue service in the U. S. and Canada, the roll call of locomotives returned to life by the railroads, museums, and dedicated volunteers has grown constantly. Train-watchers know them by initials and wheel arrangements and numbers: UP Challenger 3985, L&N 4-6-2 152, Reading 4-8-4 2102, CP Royal Hudson 2860, Frisco 4-8-2 1522, Pennsy K4 Pacific 1361, SP 4-8-4 4449, Nickel Plate Berkshire 765, CN 4-8-4 6060, Cotton Belt 4-8-4 819, SP&S 4-8-4 700. And by steam's presence, train-watchers and all who hear the steam locomotive whistle are made the richer.

Behemoths! ABOVE: Filling the blue Wyoming sky with fragrant coal smoke, Union Pacific 4-6-6-4 3985 leads an October 19, 1985, excursion over UP's main near Laramie. Alco-built Challenger 3985 was restored to service in 1981 after 22 years of silence. RIGHT: Built in Norfolk & Western's Roanoke (Virginia) Shops in 1943, N&W 1218 is the giant of Norfolk Southern's steam program. In 1987, the year it was returned to service, the 2-6-6-4 pounds former Southern rails at Cooks Springs, Alabama, with an April 21 ferry run. Both photos: David M. Johnston.

1218
1218

Norfolk Southern's steam stable. RIGHT: On her maiden public excursion run, an April 25, 1987, Roanoke-Bluefield (West Virginia) turn, N&W 1218 ignores foul weather to roll east at Ada, West Virginia. Photo: Ron Flanary. BELOW: Returned to service in 1986, Norfolk & Western's stylish Roanoke-built J-class 4-8-4 611 leads an autumn excursion over Wells Viaduct, on the old Southern Railway at Toccoa, Georgia, October 29, 1988. Photo: Steve Glischinski.

Hauling a September 8, 1985, excursion on Chicago & North Western, Nickel Plate Berkshire 765 crosses the Turtle River at Tiffany, Wisconsin. The Lima 2-8-4 was returned to service in 1979 by the Ft. Wayne (Indiana) Railroad Historical Society. Photo: Mel Finzer.

SOUTHERN PACIFIC

Restored to life in 1975 for use on the American Freedom Train (part of the nation's bicentennial), then repainted in 1984 in its famed Daylight livery, Southern Pacific GS-4 4449 has seen frequent service since. On June 19, 1984, 4449 revisits familiar territory, rolling along the Pacific Ocean on SP's Coast Line at Gaviota, California. Photo: David R. Busse.

Built by Rogers in 1905 and restored to service by the Kentucky Railway Museum 80 years later, Louisville & Nashville 4-6-2 152 bursts from Bee Rock Tunnel, October 11, 1986, on CSX trackage in eastern Virginia. Photo: Ron Flanary.

Narrow gauge gems. ABOVE: On Rio Grande's famed 45-mile Silverton branch, Durango & Silverton Narrow Gauge 2-8-2 481 reveals the glory of the Colorado Rockies to excursionists. The Durango & Silverton took over operation of this line from D&RGW in 1981. Photo: Mike Danneman. BELOW: Diminutive 2-8-2s of the East Broad Top assemble at Orbisonia, Pennsylvania, October 11, 1986. Until its 1956 shutdown EBT was the last three-foot-gauge common carrier in the U. S. east of the Mississippi River; in 1960 it reopened to haul tourists. Photo: Reid McNaught.

9 RAILS IN THE CITIES

High drama in grand urban theaters

IN U.S. AND CANADIAN CITIES railroading takes on a character seldom seem elsewhere: It is condensed, concentrated, and often supercharged with action. Urban railroading means multiple tracks woven through brick and concrete and glass landscapes, montages of red and green and yellow signals to guide trains safely through the steel mazes, great terminal stations, sprawling yards, and the constant motion of men and machines.

That railroading should be alive in the cities is hardly surprising; after all, rail transportation was devised to bring the resources of the hinterlands to the urban industries and marketplaces that require them. And railroading's tight bond with the cities is true in the human sense as well. Amtrak, VIA, and the commuter roads deliver us into the hearts of North American cities, then return us home.

Railroading's urban faces take many forms and suit many purposes. In the sprawling New Jersey terminals across the Hudson from New York City; in Long Beach, California; in

ABOVE: A Metro-North M2 electric and Amtrak AEM7 902 meet on the Northeast Corridor at New Haven, Connecticut, April 12, 1991. Photo: Gary W. Dolzall. RIGHT: Westbound Union Pacific Dash 8-40CW 9381 encounters aging Kansas City Terminal EMD SW1200s near Kansas City Union Station, September 14, 1990. Photo: Mike Danneman.

UNION PACIFIC
9381
9381
9381
6002
72

ABOVE: Departing South Station, MBTA F40PH-2C hauls commuters below the evolving skyline of Boston, January 19, 1988. Photo: Mel Finzer. BELOW: Burlington Northern intermodal train 12 threads through downtown Seattle, as it begins its long journey to Chicago. Photo: Ben Bachman. RIGHT: Set against the magnificent Statue of Liberty and lower Manhattan's brilliant skyline, New York Cross Harbor Railroad Alco S1 25 sleeps away the night at Greenville, New Jersey. Photo: Alan Tillotson.

Tacoma, Washington; in Halifax, Nova Scotia; in Vancouver, British Columbia, trains bring containers and hopper cars to exchange cargoes with the oceangoing vessels that link North America with the world. Cities like Chicago and Kansas City and Winnipeg are routing centers, melding and interchanging coal and grain and timber and intermodal traffic in every direction. In huge yards named Corwith and Queensgate and Conway and Northtown the railroads sort and block freight, load and unload trailers and containers, and tend their big diesels.

Although passenger service exists on little more than 15 percent of North America's route miles, the big cities are the stages where passenger railroading puts on its greatest show. Intercity and commuter trains are ushered in and out of 30th Street Station (Philadelphia), Penn Station (New York), Windsor Station (Montreal), and South Station (Boston). And if one kind of service symbolizes big-city railroading, it is the commuter train, whether it be the electric m.u. cars and diesel push-pulls of Long Island or the F40-led bilevels and ex-Illinois Central electrics of Metra or the Fs and Geeps and single-level coaches of Montreal's MUCTC.

For train-watchers, modern railroading in the cities calls up images of Amtrak or Burlington Northern or Conrail diesels against the Chicago skyline, of a New York Cross Harbor Railroad switcher

RIGHT: The twin towers of New York City's World Trade Center are visible in the distance as Amtrak E60 601 hurries a Northeast Corridor New York-Philadelphia *Clocker* over the Hackensack River at Kearny, New Jersey, June 26, 1990. Photo: Scott Hartley.

sleeping away the night on the Jersey side, with the distant Manhattan skyline and Statue of Liberty behind; of Terminal Railroad Association's red switchers tugging transfer freight in the shadow of the St. Louis arch; of Santa Fe piggybacks twisting through the brick canyons of Kansas City toward Argentine Yard; of BN Cascade green diesels set against the white spires of downtown Seattle. The urban scene includes the bustle of passengers at Grand Central Terminal and Toronto Union Station, and the urgent passage of scores of commuter trains in cities and suburbs from Newton, Massachusetts, to Highlands, Illinois, to San Jose, California. North America's cities are a grand urban theater in which to stage railroading's captivating drama.

Still wearing Seaboard System livery, CSX B36-7 5898 snakes a piggyback train out of Cincinnati, Ohio, toward an Ohio River bridge crossing into Kentucky, July 27, 1990. Photo: Steve Glischinski.

Southern Pacific EMD diesels of two generations congregate under a night sky alive with a summer electrical storm at SP's Taylor Yard in Los Angeles, August 6, 1990. Photo: James A. Speaker.

2196
2196
UNION PACIFIC
SOUTHLAND
Pearl Light
2196
UNION PACIFIC

PRECEDING PAGES: Union Pacific GP38-2 2196 and a GP15 — both ex-Missouri Pacific units — tug tonnage through the ultramodern urban setting of Dallas in November 1988. Another symbol of today's Texas passes overhead — a Southwest Airlines Boeing 737. Photo: Dan Pope.

RIGHT: Ditch lights shining, brilliant red CP Rail MLW M636 4711 glides past a pair of FP7s of the Montreal Urban Community Transportation Commission at Dorion, Quebec, January 14, 1990. BELOW LEFT: At Montreal's Taschereau Yard, smoky Canadian National MLW S13 switchers and slugs top the hump, August 30, 1990. Two photos: Scott Hartley. BELOW RIGHT: Far from home rails, Ontario Northland FP7 1985 heads the ex-Trans Europe Express trainset of the Toronto-North Bay-Timmins ONR *Northlander* at Toronto, August 8, 1985. The train operates 228 miles on CN trackage to link Toronto with ONR at North Bay, Ontario. Photo: Alan Tillotson.

4711

Sheraton Centre
1985
Northlander

D6
D7
2 MPH
290 290
Amtrak
195 195
Amtrak
209 209
Amtrak
392 392
Amtrak

Chicagoland. LEFT: Amtrak 195, an ex-GO Transit GP40TC, is surrounded by F40PHs at Amtrak's 14th Street shops, March 25, 1989. Photo: Mark Danneman. ABOVE: At a location that sees over 150 trains each weekday — Indiana Harbor Belt's underpass below Burlington Northern's three-track main at Congress Park, Illinois — a pair of Belt Railway of Chicago Alco C424s leads a transfer south in November 1986. Photo: Gary W. Dolzall.

Amtrak GP40TC 193 leaves downtown Milwaukee, hurrying south over snow-dusted Soo Line (ex-Milwaukee Road) rails, bound for Chicago Union Station with a three-car *LaSalle*, February 27, 1990. Photo: Mel Finzer.

Chicago & North Western SD18s (in this case, deturbocharged ex-Southern Railway SD24s) roll across the Robert Street lift bridge over the Mississippi at St. Paul, Minnesota, September 1, 1990. Photo: Steve Glischinski.

Leading a transfer cut of piggybacks to Burlington Northern's Denver intermodal terminal, venerable, white-faced BN SD9 6217 strolls through Denver, July 7, 1989. Photo: Mike Danneman.

10 MOUNTAIN RAILROADING

Titanic battles fought amid magnificent beauty

SINCE RAILS FIRST began to stretch across North America, nothing has so fiercely defied the men who built the railroads — or so challenged the trains that followed — as the great mountain ranges of the continent. No other single theme of railroading has so captivated railroaders and train-watchers as conquering the ranges; no other single element of railroading has become so rich in lore.

The places where trains and mountains clash are now names of legend: Horse Shoe Curve, Tehachapi Loop, Allegheny Mountain, Sand Patch Grade, Soldier Summit, the Fraser River Canyon, Magnolia Cutoff, Saluda Grade, and Cumberland Mountain. Famous passes — Rogers, Marias, Donner, and Tennessee — and famous tunnels — Big Bend, Hoosac, Cascade, and Moffat — punctuate the mountain crossings.

ABOVE: Appalachian drama. Running on Norfolk Southern via trackage rights, CSX trains meet at Jasper, Virginia, August 14, 1987. Photo: Ron Flanary. RIGHT: The magnificent Canadian Rockies. Near Lake Louise at the western edge of Alberta, CP Rail SDs guide an intermodal train along the Bow River, August 5, 1989. Photo: Alan Tillotson.

5901
5901
CP Rail
5901
5702

It's June 3, 1989, but snow lingers high on Donner Pass as four Southern Pacific EMDs headed by SD40T-2 8336 ease a grain train down the west slope near Yuba Pass, California. Photo: Alex Mayes.

It is easy to understand the timeless appeal of trains in the mountains: Railroad versus mountain is, in the truest sense, a battle of titans. Unforgiving rock cliffs and gorges and grades are pitted against men and machines determined to lift coal and ore and grain and containers up and over the Berkshires, the Blue Ridge, the Wasatch, the Selkirks.

The battle is joined in scores of locations. It awaits us in the Appalachians of Virginia, where Norfolk Southern's black beasts drag strings of hoppers up to Montgomery Tunnel; it awaits on the slopes of Donner Pass, at Norden and Andover and Truckee, where SP's scarlet and gray EMDs howl against snowy slopes; it awaits deep among the rock cliffs of the Breaks of the Big Sandy River, where CSX GEs lead coal hoppers along the old Clinchfield main; it awaits at Field, British Columbia, where Canadian Pacific SD40-2s dig in and begin their struggle against gravity up the 2.2 percent grades of the west slope of Kicking Horse Pass.

And while much of the appeal of mountain railroading is in these epic battles, the battlefields present train-watchers with unrivaled beauty. Amtrak's *California Zephyr* rolls alongside the rushing waters of the Colorado River, a silver necklace set against the sheer cliffs of Glenwood Canyon; blue Conrail diesels curl around Horse Shoe as dawn touches the Allegheny Mountains with fingers of sunlight; the snowy peaks of the Montana Rockies glitter white as a Burlington Northern intermodal climbs Marias Pass; a Montana Rail Link freight twists gracefully around the horseshoe curves of Mullan Pass, blue diesels set against evergreen slopes; CSX diesels roar amid the bright shades of autumn foliage drawing freight over the ancient, cinder-dusted route that is Sand Patch Grade; red, white, and blue British Columbia Railway diesels twist along the Squamish River, clinging to stone ledges to squeeze through the Coast Mountains.

In all of train-watching there is no more worthy an endeavor than to stand trackside and listen to the desperate battle of diesels lifting a heavy train toward a mountain summit. First ever-so-distant, then slowly drawing closer, we hear — and feel — the thunder of four or five or six locomotives, 12,000 horsepower, perhaps more, grinding up grade, spitting sand for traction. The great iron creatures roll past, headlights searching the rocky crags, turbochargers pulsing out black, swirling exhaust. Like other great battles fought by men and machine, the memories of these encounters can linger forever — and touch the train-watcher's soul.

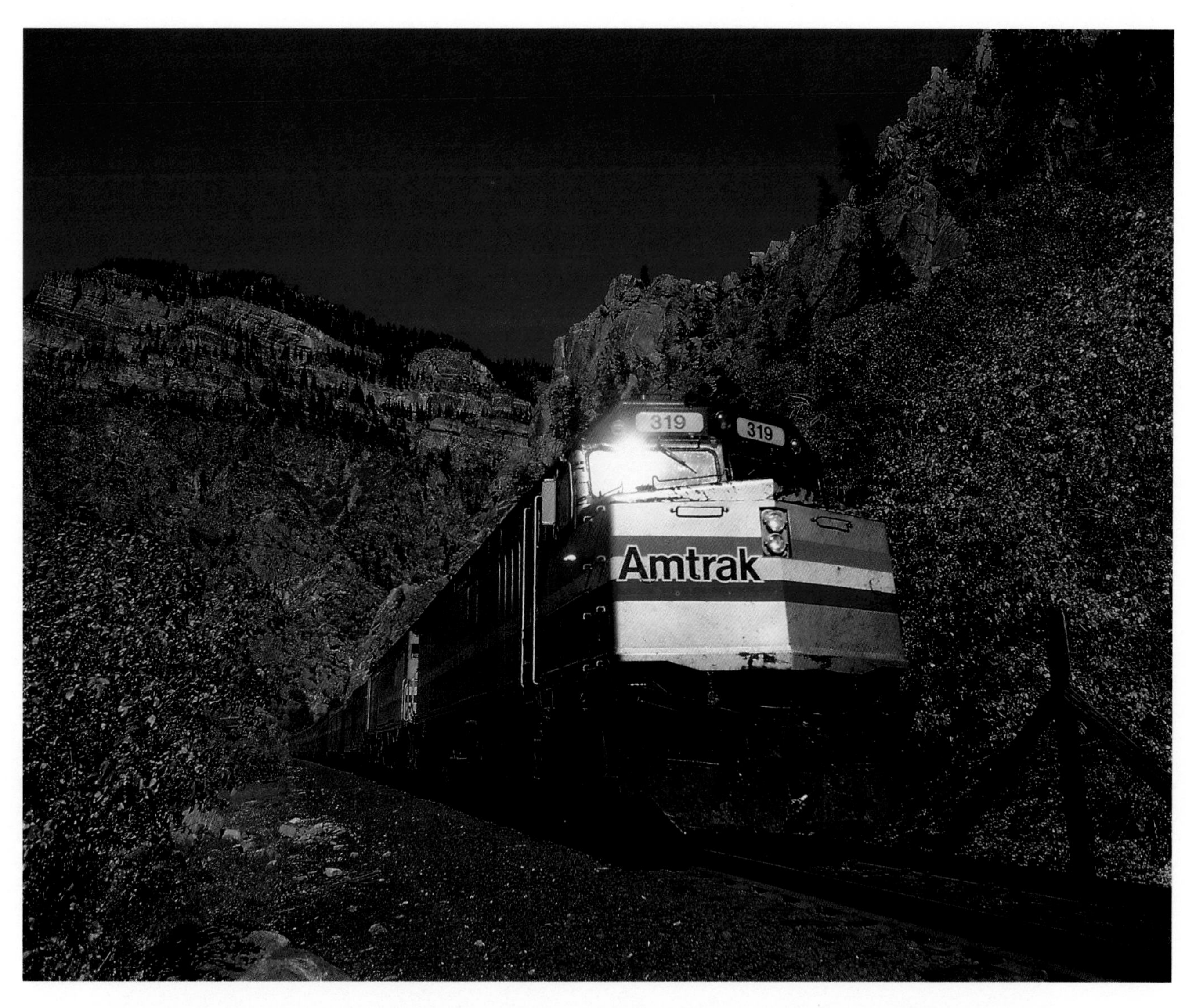

Sunshine reflects from the windshield of Amtrak F40PH 319 as the westbound *California Zephyr* traces Rio Grande's rails through deep Glenwood Canyon, east of Glenwood Springs, Colorado, September 28, 1987. Photo: James A. Speaker.

Tehachapi! Built to link the Mojave desert and California's Bay area in 1875-1876, Southern Pacific's line over the Tehachapi Mountains — shared since 1899 with Santa Fe — is one of North America's railroad marvels. BELOW: At the crown jewel of the mountain crossing — Tehachapi Loop at Walong, California — an eastbound Santa Fe piggyback wraps over itself, April 6, 1990. Photo: Ron Flanary. RIGHT: Southern Pacific SD45 7550 clears Tunnel 9 at Walong as an SP freight negotiates the Loop, April 3, 1990. Photo: Ron Flanary. ABOVE: Only three miles from Walong, a quartet of Santa Fe GE Dash 8-40Bs urges intermodal loads eastbound at Woodford, California, November 7, 1990. Photo: Don R. Flynn.

CP Rail
SOUTHERN PACIFIC
7550
7550
SP

311
311
Amtrak

LEFT: The Alleghenies in Pennsylvania. At Mapleton, where Conrail's ex-Pennsylvania Railroad Middle Division main squeezes between the canyon walls of Jacks Mountain, Amtrak's eastbound *Broadway Limited* ducks under a traditional PRR signal bridge behind a pair of F40PHs, June 11, 1989. BELOW LEFT: Fingers of dawn brighten the autumn shades of the Alleghenies as Conrail SD40s push westbound tonnage up Horse Shoe Curve, west of Altoona, October 23, 1988. BELOW: A CSX freight fights tonnage and wet rail in a cold pouring rain at Keystone, October 22, 1988. Only one mile ahead is the town which gives this ex-B&O mountain crossing its name — Sand Patch. Three photos: Gary W. Dolzall.

CP Rail
CP Rail
CP Rail

PRECEDING PAGES: CP Rail SD40s roll tonnage west along the Kicking Horse River at Glenogle, British Columbia, October 1, 1989, amid the beauty — and drama — of CP's legendary crossing of the Canadian Rockies. Photo: Steve Patterson.

"Main line thru the Rockies." ABOVE: Rio Grande's longtime slogan still applies, although its image is changing: Witness a trio of Southern Pacific diesels headed by SD40 7304 guiding westbound tonnage over D&RGW's Tennessee Pass near Pando, Colorado, September 22, 1989. Photo: Blair Kooistra. RIGHT: Eastbound Rio Grande GP40-2 3099 and a sister pop out of Tunnel 5 on D&RGW's Moffat line through the Front Range, June 29, 1989. Photo: Steve Patterson.

Great Northern mountain legacy. To link Chicago and Seattle, Burlington Northern must negotiate two great mountain crossings engineered by James J. Hill's Great Northern. ABOVE: Four BN EMDs tote stacks through the Montana Rockies on Marias Pass, July 21, 1990. Photo: Tom Danneman. RIGHT: BN GP39-2s and GEs guide stacks through Marias below the snowy peaks of Glacier National Park, March 3, 1989. Photo: Mike Danneman. BELOW: Farther west, GP39-2 2710 works through Stevens Pass, BN's crossing of the Cascades, at Index, Washington, in December 1985. Photo: Ben Bachman.

2709
2709
2700
8513

ABOVE: Grandeur lost. Eighteen months before its January 1990 discontinuance, VIA Rail's *Canadian* attains Partridge, British Columbia, on CP Rail's main line through the Rockies. Photo: Ron Cady. ABOVE RIGHT: Few North American mountain passes are more famous than California's Cajon. Santa Fe and Union Pacific share trackage through the pass, and SP's Colton-Palmdale Cutoff is present as well. On January 10, 1987, a quartet of Santa Fe six-axle GEs urges heavy eastbound tonnage through Cajon. Photo: David R. Busse. BELOW RIGHT: Union Pacific Dash 8-40Cs roll American President Lines stacks over Cajon, June 24, 1989. Photo: George W. Hamlin.

8129
Santa Fe

9135
9135
UNION PACIFIC

LEFT: Norfolk Southern SDs prepare to plunge into Virginia's 850-foot Natural Tunnel, October 26, 1990. This former Southern line between Frisco, Tennessee, and Big Stone Gap, Virginia, hosts both NS and CSX tonnage. Photo: Katie Kern. ABOVE: Rolling down the east slope of Washington Hill at Middlefield, Massachusetts, Conrail C30-7As lead train TV6 over the Berkshires, October 7, 1990. Photo: Scott Hartley. BELOW: Age-old Delaware & Hudson wears a changed face as SD40s of new owner CP Rail roll out of Belden Hill Tunnel, north of Binghamton, New York, October 3, 1990. Photo: Alan Tillotson.

Union Pacific's grand West. ABOVE: On the former Western Pacific steel trail through California's Feather River Canyon, Union Pacific SD60M 6197 and two GEs head stacks east over Clio Trestle, October 20, 1990. Photo: Steve Schmollinger. ABOVE RIGHT: East of Ogden in Utah's Echo Canyon, Dash 8-40C 9130 guides stacks along UP's Overland Route, February 6, 1988. Photo: Blair Kooistra. BELOW: UP SD40-2s are silhouetted against the distant, snow-dressed Pilot Range as tonnage moves east through Clifside, Nevada, on the old WP, February 5, 1990. Photo: Blair Kooistra.

9130
9130
9130
UNION PACIFIC
9109

100
100
Santa Fe
100
SANTA FE
Santa Fe

11 RAILS ACROSS THE CONTINENT

Captivating scenes and changing moods

WHAT CALLS US TO TRACKSIDE? Why does railroading so captivate us? The answer for each of us will be different, as different as the blistering pace of Amtrak AEM7s on the Northeast Corridor is from the lonely wanderings of a Canadian National Geep with a single car of Manitoba grain. But whether it's Santa Fe GEs drawing piggybacks over the Arizona Divide or Burlington Northern diesels tugging tonnage along the banks of the Mississippi River, whether it's a Dash 8-40C or a 4-8-4, the appeal is there.

Surely much of what is intriguing in the railroad scene is in the way its purposes and faces change. Across North America railroads have, for a century and a half, called boys — and grown-up boys — to trackside. One day the experience is the angular steel face and slapping exhaust of a Susquehanna Dash 8-40B, the next it's the friendly human

LEFT: Warbonnets in Cajon! Freshly repainted in Santa Fe's famed Warbonnet scheme, FP45s lead stacks through Cajon Pass, California, August 10, 1989. Photo: David R. Busse. ABOVE: Chicagoland commuter. Metra F40PH 134 glides west on the Chicago & North Western at Elmhurst, Illinois, March 5, 1988. Photo: Gary W. Dolzall.

face and soft voice of a talkative tower operator. The contrasts continue: The careful pace of Canadian National RSC14s across Nova Scotia's grasslands is a far cry from the raspy voice and booming whistle of Union Pacific 3985 atop Wyoming's high plains. Railroading can awe us with the engineering accomplishment of Copper Creek trestle or the Spiral Tunnels, or comfort us with the anticipation of a warm, snug roomette in an Amtrak sleeping car as we stand waiting on a chilly, windy station platform at Manassas, Virginia.

That railroading plays its drama across the vast natural amphitheater of this continent gives it diversity — but also a home-town familiarity, whether home is Bangor, Maine, or Windsor, Ontario, or Bakersfield, California. Railroading, like a good friend, can always be found, whether in the yards at Cumberland, Maryland, or at Tower 55 in Fort Worth, or on the SP steel that traces California's Pacific coast. Railroading carries on, day and night, in every season, in all weather, and shows us ever-changing moods and images. Whether the sights and sounds are of a Conrail freight appearing out of the golden dusk of an Indiana summer evening; of BN Marias Pass pushers huddled against the cold of a snowy night at Essex, Montana; of NS diesels coasting through the fog of an Appalachian morning; or of UP SD60s fending off the 100-degree temperatures of the Utah desert, we have ample reason to return, time and time again, to seek the spirit of railroading.

The distant San Francisco Peaks frame Santa Fe Dash 8-40B 7439 as it crosses the 7,000-foot-elevation Arizona Divide west of Flagstaff, at dusk, April 20, 1990. Photo: Mike Danneman.

ABOVE: In the Meadow Valley of southeast Nevada near Elgin, a trio of Union Pacific GEs headed by C36-7 9017 rolls west toward Las Vegas and eventually Los Angeles, September 14, 1989. Photo: Mel Finzer. BELOW: Near Germantown, Wisconsin, two ex-Burlington SD24s and an ex-Southern SD35 of regional Fox River Valley Railroad roll north on former Chicago & North Western rails, March 25, 1990. Photo: Gary W. Dolzall.

In the golden glow of an Indian summer evening, Conrail EMDs roll east across northern Indiana, near Otis on the former New York Central main line, October 9, 1988. Photo: Gary W. Dolzall.

LEFT: Burlington Northern 2006 — an EMD GP20 rebuilt in 1989 with a Caterpillar diesel engine — cruises along the east bank of the Mississippi at Genoa, Wisconsin, July 1, 1990, at the head of Chicago-bound BN intermodal train 2. Photo: Gary W. Dolzall.

BELOW: At dusk, clouds swirl in the desert sky as Southern Pacific SD40T-2 8361 stands near the Tehachapi Mountains at Mojave, California, February 28, 1988. Photo: Mike Danneman.

RIGHT: The last hints of autumn foliage dress the hills of Anthonys Nose, New York, as a venerable Metro-North FL9 follows the east bank of the Hudson River near Bear Mountain Bridge with a New York City-to-Poughkeepsie (New York) commuter train, November 11, 1990. Photo: Gary W. Dolzall.

Where Amtrak's *San Diegan* passenger trains are a more common sight than tonnage, Santa Fe GP35 2804 leads freight along the Pacific shore at San Clemente, California. Photo: David R. Busse.

Against the background of Jones & Laughlin Steel's aged mill, CSX GP40s in Chessie System colors thread a string of box cars through Pittsburgh, June 17, 1988. Photo: Mel Finzer.

ABOVE: The trains of two railroads which disappeared only to reappear — Illinois Central and Toledo, Peoria & Western — cross paths at Gilman, Illinois, May 5, 1990. The two-tone gray livery of westbound TP&W GP20 2001 is a reincarnation of New York Central's old scheme. Photo: Gary W. Dolzall. ABOVE RIGHT: Another transformation in the Midwest is evident as Cotton Belt B30-7 7770 passes through Wilmington, Illinois, June 30, 1990, on what was once Gulf, Mobile & Ohio's Chicago-St. Louis main. Cotton Belt took over this line from regional Chicago, Missouri & Western in 1989, giving parent Southern Pacific its long-sought entrance into Chicago. Photo: H. Michael Yuhas. BELOW RIGHT: On the New York & Long Branch, once shared by the trains of Pennsy and Jersey Central, NJ Transit F40PH 4127 rolls across the Raritan River at Perth Amboy, New Jersey, August 31, 1986. Photo: Alan Tillotson.

WILMINGTON
7770
7770
7770

4127
NJ TRANSIT

NW

PRECEDING PAGES: In one of eastern railroading's grandest settings — Portage Bridge over the Genesee River at Letchworth State Park, New York — Susquehanna and Delaware & Hudson diesels roll D&H tonnage west toward Buffalo in September 1989. This is Conrail's Southern Tier Line, over which D&H (now Canadian Pacific) has trackage rights. Photo: John S. Murray.

Away from home rails, Guilford (Boston & Maine) GP39-2 364 leads mixed freight and empty coal hoppers bound west from a New Hampshire utility over Pittsburgh & Lake Erie rails at Pittsburgh. Photo: John S. Murray.

ABOVE: Amid Wisconsin's winter fury, workmen clear switches at Chicago & North Western's Butler yard while two trains and the yard switcher — Geep 4105 — look on, December 3, 1990. Photo: Mike Danneman. BELOW: In a scene rich in railroad tradition, Amtrak's *Crescent* prepares to stop at Manassas, Virginia, on the former Southern Railway main, December 2, 1989. Photo: George W. Hamlin.

Curving through Midwestern farmland, the containers of a westbound Burlington Northern intermodal trail BN Cascade Green EMDs near Shabbona, Illinois, October 19, 1990. Photo: Vern Finzer and Mel Finzer.

ABOVE: The steel trail is the ex-Milwaukee Road Chicago-Twin Cities main line, but the image is far removed from the days of orange and black as wide-nose Soo SD60M 6059 bends westbound tonnage through a curve at Delafield, Wisconsin, August 9, 1990. Photo: Mike Danneman. BELOW: A Santa Fe eastbound freight wraps itself along the slopes of the Tehachapi Mountains at Bealville, California, February 10, 1990. Photo: Steve Patterson.

On the former Great Northern at Newport, Washington, Burlington Northern GP9s which once served Northern Pacific trundle along the Pend Oreille River with an eastbound local, July 20, 1989. Photo: Dave Gayer.

RIGHT: CSX SD50s draw hoppers south across one of the landmarks of the Clinchfield Railroad — majestic Copper Creek Viaduct at Speer's Ferry, Virginia — October 26, 1990. The line at the base of the viaduct belongs to Norfolk Southern, and by trackage rights agreements either road's trains may be seen above or below. Photo: Mike Danneman.

BELOW: BC Rail MLW M630 722 swings past the water tower at Lone Butte, British Columbia, dragging freight south toward North Vancouver, August 31, 1986. Photo: Steve Glischinski.

Corridor speedster. Amtrak AEM7 918 races along the former New Haven portion of the Northeast Corridor, hustling train 85 — *The Virginian* — through Westport, Connecticut, February 9, 1991. Photo: Gary W. Dolzall.

ACKNOWLEDGMENTS

IN CLOSING OUR FIRST BOOK on contemporary railroading (*Steel Rails Across America*, Kalmbach, 1989) we reserved our first thanks for our contributing photographers, noting that without their enthusiastic support and the extraordinary camera work they provided, the book would not have been possible. That statement holds even more true for this volume, and, again, we express our deepest appreciation to all who contributed images to this book.

We are proud that many of the same skilled lensmen who aided our first effort were key contributors to this book. In addition to the authors', the following photographers' work is represented: Scott Hartley, Mel Finzer, Ron Flanary, Steve Patterson, Alan Tillotson, John Murray, Blair Kooistra, Alex Mayes, Dave Gayer, George Hamlin, Steve Glischinski, Mark Wayman, Don Flynn, Ben Bachman, David Johnston, Mark Danneman, Tom Danneman, Ron Cady, Mike Small, Robert Palmer, Reid McNaught, James Speaker, H. Michael Yuhas, Katie Kern, Steve Schmollinger, Dave Busse, Dan Pope, and Mark Lynn.

In addition, we thank all who gave us support and advice throughout the preparation of this book, especially our families and loved ones, and, in particular, Mark and Tom Danneman (Mike's brothers), who assisted in design, and Donnette Dolzall (Gary's wife) for manuscript editing.

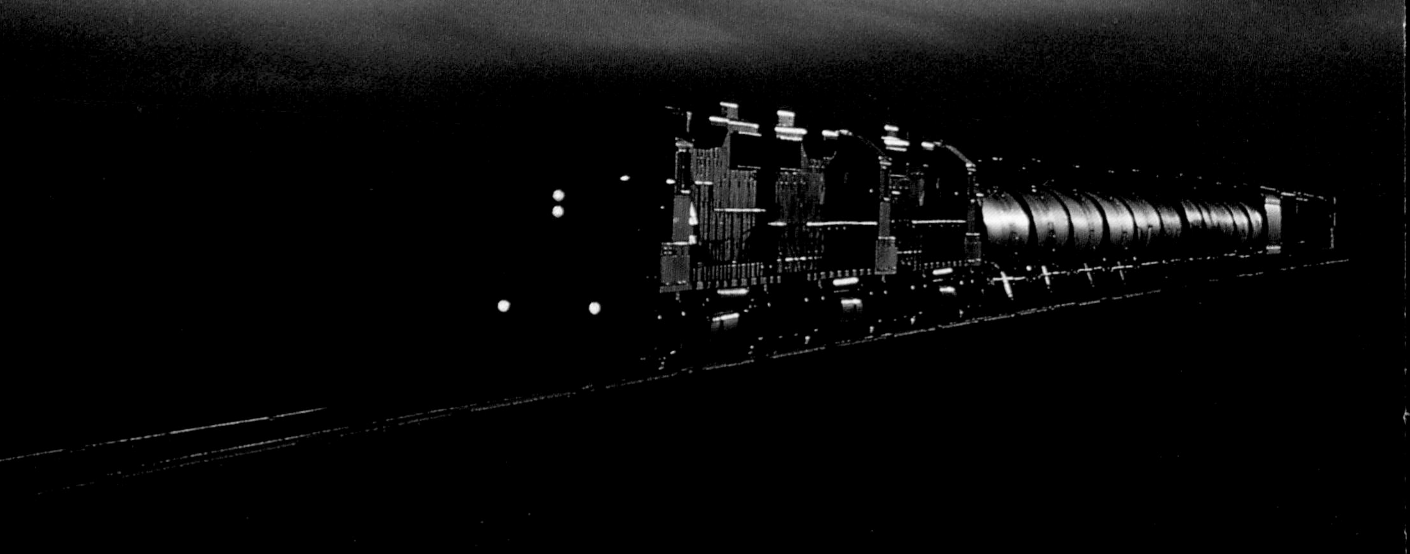

Revealing all that is the enduring spirit of railroading, CP Rail GP38s march across endless plains at Cosway Junction, Alberta, November 29, 1990. Photo: Mel Finzer.